Vegan Delights

Vegan Delights

88 Delicious Recipes for the Complete Three-Course Meal

Toni Rodríguez

Skyhorse Publishing

Skyhorse Publishing books may be purchased in bulk at special discounts for sales promotion, corporate gifts, fund-raising, or educational purposes. Special editions can also be created to specifications. For details, contact the Special Sales Department, Skyhorse Publishing, 307 West 36th Street, 11th Floor, New York, NY 10018 or info@skyhorsepublishing.com.

Skyhorse® and Skyhorse Publishing® are registered trademarks of Skyhorse Publishing, Inc.®, a Delaware corporation.

Visit our website at www.skyhorsepublishing.com.

10 9 8 7 6 5 4 3 2 1

Library of Congress Cataloging-in-Publication Data is available on file.

Cover design by Erin Seaward-Hiatt
Cover photo credit Becky Lawton

Print ISBN: 978-1-63450-457-7
Ebook ISBN: 978-1-63450-475-1

Printed in China

*Because the main ingredient of every recipe is love,
this is for all the people who love animals and
enjoy good cooking.*

Contents

Eat, drink, enjoy

More than ten years ago, I stopped eating animals. It took me a long time to realize that eating muscle, membranes, and other products was just something I enjoyed . . . but that it was costing the lives of those animals that were arriving at my plate. Now that I think about it, how could I feel pleasure while eating the organs of animals instead of tomatoes, tofu, hummus, or pesto? I must have been crazy then, or maybe the craze actually came to me ten years ago. Surely, being different and feeling intense empathy for animals must be a beautiful kind of insanity.

I haven't given up on pleasure. In fact, I think that deep down I am a hedonist. I am always searching for new flavors, I prefer to have a bit of sun on my face, traveling rather than staying put, eating, drinking, enjoying . . . perhaps that's why I start salivating when I open the book that you are now holding in your hands.

I've known Toni since he was 17 years old, when he dreamed of becoming a rock star. We both stopped eating animals because we believe that they have the same right as we do to not be devoured and to enjoy their lives peacefully and freely. We believe this in our heads and hearts, and these recipes lead us to believe with our palates that there is no reason to continue sending animals to the slaughterhouse.

This book contains more than just recipes. Its pages are filled with loving encounters, picnic outings, formal dinners, games, and gifts. They contain an infinite number of enjoyable scenarios, without even a shadow of suffering.

Francisco Vásquez Neira
Co-founder of AnimaNaturalis Internacional

Cooking is love

My father taught me a guiding principle: "You must work hard to obtain what you want." Work and . . . lots of love. Because the main ingredient of every recipe is love, there is an affection that you impart while making it. In fact, I began cooking because of love. My partner, also vegan, couldn't do it because of work, and from there I found a new passion: wholesome cooking.

I am vegan for ethical reasons. I refuse to eat anything that involves the mistreatment of animals. My recipes do not use any ingredients that come from animals (meat, milk, eggs, honey). If cooking is love, there can be no suffering involved.

As a vegan chef, I am always excited to try new things in the kitchen. This book is a good example. In these pages you will find a great number of original, fun, and easy to prepare recipes. You'll discover new textures, new flavors, new ways of preparing one hundred percent healthy and natural ingredients.

I hope you enjoy and that your dinner guests also enjoy the offerings of *Vegan Delights*. And if you would like to try out some more recipes, don't forget to visit www.lujuriavegana.com. I'll be waiting for you there with new ideas! To finish up, I'd like to give my most sincere thanks to the whole team at Editorial Océano. Without them, this book would not have been possible. A million heartfelt thanks.

Toni Rodríguez

Vegan temptations

You can make some really good things as a vegan. This is the philosophy of Toni Rodríguez, a young and enthusiastic cook who one day left behind his job as a tech and created Lujuria Vegana—an intriguing name for a team of professionals that create and commercialize on a daily basis an innumerable amount of exquisite vegan delicacies free of any animal-based ingredients. Toni is self-taught and always experimenting with new flavors, aromas, or textures with which he astonishes a clientele that is greater and more loyal every day. He has both vegan and non-vegan clients because his innovative cakes, brownies, cookies, and pies are a delicious temptation that attracts all types: people who have high cholesterol, people with allergies to eggs and/or lactose, people who want to skip their diet without going too far, or those who simply want to try something new, surprising, and delicious.

Cravings a la carte

Toni Rodríguez's pioneering business venture started in his small home kitchen. There he experimented with all types of sweet and salty ingredients and investigated vegan alternatives to create amazing recipes. He spent many hours by the flames and, little by little, began picking up the necessary experience to realize his dream: creating the first vegan bakery and cake shop in Europe. Said and done: alongside the entrepreneurial Rosa Avellaneda, they started a professional enterprise that soon began to gather excellent reviews. His sweet offerings could not be more appetizing and suggestive: vegan cheesecake, crisp coconut cookies, raspberry brittle, chocolate bombs with peanut butter mouse and chocolate glaze, carrot cake with a vegan cheese topping . . .

A delight to the senses

The author of this book is part of a new generation of young chefs dedicated to bringing vegan cuisine to the broad public. By combining top quality raw materials with the audacity and originality of their creations, they are breathing new life into this form of cooking without animal-based ingredients.

Through this book, the young chef invites us to discover a new concept of vegan cooking with a variety of recipes that are surprising and very healthy and will be the delight of our dinner guests. A simple, fresh, and original showpiece, with a creative and innovative touch. And definitely, a vegan delight for the senses.

Where to taste the offerings of the author

Lujuria Vegana boasts a wide selection of vegan pastries that a restless Toni Rodríguez updates every season. They also supply their products to various clients such as hotels, restaurants, coffee shops, catering companies, etc.
At this time, there are several points of sale in Barcelona and the surrounding areas. They have permanent shops at Pastelería La Estrella (Nou de la Rambla, 32), Gopal (Escudellers, 42), Ecocentre Vegania (Mallorca, 330), Veganoteca (Valldonzella, 60), Obrador Lujuria Vegana (Ptge. Can Polític 19. L'Hospitalet de Llobregat) and Tot Natural (Pi i Margall, 91. Sant Boi de Llobregat). Toni Rodríguez's offerings may also be ordered by email (info@lujuriavegana.com) or through Facebook (www.facebook.com/lujuriavegana).

What are we talking about?

There are more and more people who want to reduce their consumption of animal-based foods: to avoid the exploitation of other species, for health reasons, or to reduce the environmental impact of the cattle industry. The motivations are quite varied and for this reason there are different types of vegetarianism. The one thing that all vegetarian diets have in common is the rejection of the consumption of meat, be it from birds, mammals, or fish. It's true that some people who eat fish call themselves vegetarians, but the truth is that they should be called "semivegetarians."

Generally, you can establish the following classifications according to which animal-based products a person wishes to avoid:

Vegetarian. Do not eat meat, fish, or their derived products, although they may or may not include in their diets the consumption of eggs or dairy products. The word "vegetarian" comes from the Latin *vegetus*, which means "healthy" and was officially used for the first time on the 30th of September of 1847 during the inaugural ceremony of the Vegetarian Society of the United Kingdom. Previously, people who did not eat meat were known as "Pythagoreans," in honor of the Greek philosopher Pythagoras, who is considered to be the first modern vegetarian.

Vegan. Excludes, as much as possible, every manner of exploitation and cruelty towards animals, be this food, clothing, or any other use. In culinary terms, veganism refers to the practice of eliminating all animal-based products, including meat, fish, shellfish, eggs, milk, honey, and

all their derivatives. Vegans are also known as strict vegetarians. Their precursors were Elsie Shrigley and Donald Watson, vegetarians who in 1944 founded the Vegan Society of the United Kingdom. According to Watson, "veganism is a life philosophy that excludes all forms of exploitation and cruelty towards the animal kingdom and fosters reverence for life. In practice, it is applied by following a pure vegetarian diet and it encourages the use of alternatives to all materials derived partially or completely from animals."

Ovo-lacto vegetarian. Do not eat meat, fish, or their derived products, but they eat eggs and dairy products. This is the most widespread form of vegetarianism.

Lacto-vegetarian. They do not eat meat, fish and their derived products, eggs, or any animal-based products except for dairy products.

Crudivore. They follow a vegetarian diet composed basically of uncooked fruits and vegetables.

Frugivore. They only eat fresh or dry fruits and nuts.

Macrobiotics. This group centers its diet on cereals, vegetables in season, and whole foods.

Famous vegans and Vegetarians

The world of cinema, music, and art is full of people that have adopted veganism or vegetarianism as a philosophy and style of life. Here are some of the most prominent:

- Pamela Anderson, actress
- Uma Thurman, actress
- Natalie Portman, actress
- Alanis Morissette, singer
- Bill Clinton, former president of the United States
- Brandon Flowers, vocalist of The Killers
- Steve Jobs, former executive president of Apple
- Mark Zuckerberg, creator of Facebook
- Chris Martin, vocalist of Coldplay
- Donna Karan, fashion designer
- Drew Barrymore, actress
- Fiona Apple, singer
- Jennifer Connelly, actress
- Martina Navratilova, tennis player
- Moby, musician
- Paul McCartney, musician
- Joaquin Phoenix, actor
- Prince, singer
- Sinéad O'Connor, singer
- Stella McCartney, designer
- Sting, musician

Good reasons to be vegan

Following a vegan diet with no animal-based ingredients is a whole philosophy and way of life that may be followed for different reasons. Here is a brief explanation of the main reasons.

Improving your health

According to the Academy of Nutrition and Dietetics, vegetarian diets that are adequately planned, including totally vegetarian or vegan diets, are healthy, nutritionally adequate, and can provide health benefits for the prevention and treatment of certain diseases. Well planned vegetarian diets are appropriate for every stage of life, including pregnancy, breastfeeding, infancy, childhood, adolescence, and even for athletes.

Without a doubt, vegan food is among the healthiest in existence, capable of notably reducing illnesses and health disorders. To begin with, vegans possess much lower levels of cholesterol than those who eat meat and, consequently, suffer less frequently from cardiovascular afflictions. As far as substituting animal protein for vegetable protein, it has been shown that this helps reduce the amount of cholesterol in the blood. Recent studies have also shown that a diet rich in complex carbohydrates (only obtainable from vegetable foods) and low in fat is the best medicine for controlling illnesses like diabetes. On the other hand, vegetable fats tend to reduce arterial pressure while animal fats increase it. Generally, vegans are less likely to suffer from heart conditions, as well as hypertension, obesity, diabetes, cancer, intestinal disorders, kidney and vesicle stones, and osteoporosis. Any doctor would advise following a diet low in fats and rich in fiber and vitamins.

The World Health Organization (WHO) itself recommends lowering the consumption of fats and increasing the intake of fruits, vegetables, cereals, and legumes—basic vegan foods. The antioxidants present in fruits and vegetables are essential for protecting our bodies from external aggression. On the other hand, carbohydrates are one of the body's most important sources of energy, and the vegan diet is rich in this element, thanks to the abundance of fruits, cereals, legumes, and vegetables. Finally, it is worth noting that vegetables are the foods richest in vitamins, minerals, and fiber.

Easing digestion

There are more and more people suffering from indigestion on a regular basis, most of the time as a result of a deficient diet. To avoid this, it's very important to eat a good amount of fiber. This eases the movement of digested food through the small and large intestines, as well as helping the body to absorb vitamins and minerals and to eliminate toxins. The vegan diet is ideal for regulating the correct functioning of the digestive system and avoiding problems such as being overweight or obese.

Saving money

A vegan's shopping list, full of all kinds of fruits, vegetables, cereals, and, in general, any other ingredients belonging to a vegan diet, is cheaper than that of an omnivore that includes meat, fish, shellfish, and dairy. Even so, you should follow these tips if you want to reduce your spending even further:

* **Plan your meals.** Spend 15 minutes a week to prepare a menu for the next 7 days and build a shopping list with everything you need (Sunday afternoon could be a good time to do this).

* **Trust in the basic foods of your vegan diet.** Generally, they tend to be cheaper, and their versatility allows for an infinite variation of dishes. For example, legumes are cheap, durable, and offer many combinations depending on how they are cooked and the ingredients that accompany them.

* **Buy fruits and vegetables that are in season.** Whenever you are shopping, you can always find seasonal products that are much cheaper and tastier.

* **Cook in bulk.** Once a week, plan to make a large amount of a single dish and then freeze it, so you can eat it over the course of several days. Choose ingredients that you can ration out, such as cooked beans, pasta sauces, and vegetable stock.

Reduce your excessive consumption of protein

Protein is necessary for growth and the maintenance of tissues. It is comprised of a series of amino acids necessary for the proper development of the human body. Most foods contain protein in some small or large amounts. Protein with all the essential amino acids needed by the body is known as high quality protein. Some foods have a greater amount than others, but the key is knowing how to combine them so the body receives enough of these essential amino acids. Vegans who maintain a balanced diet based on cereals, legumes, seeds, nuts, and vegetables consume a mix of high quality protein.

The ideal amount in a balanced diet should be around 15 percent protein. However, much of the time, people are eating in excess of 25 percent protein and losing out on other important nutrients like carbohydrates. The vegan diet allows one to limit the excessive consumption of protein that can be detrimental to one's health in the long run. In fact, a high intake of protein can increase the body's loss of calcium and accelerate the onset of diseases such as osteoporosis.

Respecting the planet

According to the Food and Agriculture Organization of the United Nations (FAO), the livestock sector generates more greenhouse gases than the transport sector. As such, it is also one of the leading causes of the deterioration of the ground and hydrological resources. The Food and Agriculture Organization has made it clear in one of their recent reports:

> It is expected that agricultural impacts increase substantially as a result of demographic growth, increasing the consumption of animal products. Unlike fossil fuels, it is hard to find alternatives: people have to eat. A substantial reduction of these impacts can only be made possible with a substantial change in the whole world's eating habits, steering far away from animal-based products.

It is clear that reducing or completely eliminating the consumption of meat and its derivatives is a move that could contribute to reducing our ecological footprint on the planet.

Vegan resources rich in protein

- Cereals like oats, rice, buckwheat, or derived products such as pasta and bread.
- Legumes like garbanzos, beans, lentils, and soybeans.
- Nuts like walnuts, hazelnuts, almonds, and cashews.
- Sunflower, pumpkin, and sesame seeds.

Avoiding animal suffering

Many people turn to veganism because of an ethical conviction against the intense breeding techniques imposed on present day livestock. Animals destined to be food are excluded from laws against animal cruelty and receive no legal protection. As vegans, we can contribute to lowering the impact of this situation and avoid the exploitation, suffering, and sacrifice of many species of animals destined for human consumption.

Veganism is a lifestyle based on respect for animals. Vegans advocate applying to all animal species the same human rights that defend the right to life, personal safety, and freedom from slavery and torture. As a result, these obligations and rights prevent the consumption of animal-based products. The current exploitation that animals suffer at the hands of different sectors such as the food industry, fashion industry, cosmetics, etc., is considered by veganism to be a violation of rights and a state of being comparable to slavery.

Animal rights defense movements report that on a daily basis millions of species are bought, sold, deprived of freedom, taken from their families, artificially inseminated, or sacrificed, all to benefit the economic interests of industry. When we eat, when we dress, when we use products that have been tested on animals, we are contributors to their suffering and torture.

Animal rights groups insist upon the need for society to be conscious that all animals that possess a nervous system (human beings, dogs, pigs, cows, chickens, tunas, rats, etc.) have the capability to feel (be it pain, pleasure, or fear) and that, as such, also have the same needs and should be respected. These same groups advocate to eradicate speciesism, or discrimination on the basis of species.

Speciesism establishes a hierarchical order for the importance of the needs of one determined species over another. For example, we are speciesist when we give priority to the needs of a dog over the needs of a cow or pig. This culture hides the fact that human beings are also animals and that they do not have the right to own the life of their non-human fellows. It is clear that we are different, but what animal rights movements denounce is that those differences give us the right to dominate other species. They reject the self-awarded "right" of humans to treat other species as mere objects that exist simply to satisfy our own desires and serve as a means to reach our own goals. According to the philosopher José Ferrater Mora, "speciesism is to the entire human species what racism is to a single specific race. Being speciesist is being human racist. The appreciation of the human being as a species becomes speciesism when it equates itself to the denial of the rights of other species, but not those of humans."

To avoid this discrimination (equal to both sexism and racism in its injustice), this movement promotes veganism as being the only valid choice. This involves avoiding the use of animals in any aspect of life by committing to a one hundred percent vegetarian diet (no dairy products, eggs, or honey); choosing clothes and accessories that do not have leather, wool, or silk; not using animal-tested products; boycotting zoos and aquariums; as well as not participating in parties or shows where other animals are used for entertaining or amusing the public.

Some victims of speciesism

- **Animals sacrificed by the fur industry.** This business sacrifices an enormous amount of animal species on a daily basis to make all kinds of coats and other clothing items. Mink, chinchillas, adult and baby seals, otters, foxes, pine martens, squirrels, and other animals die cruelly every day to avoid any imperfection in the appearance of their skin.
- **Sacrifice and exploitation of cows.** Bovine livestock is submitted on a daily basis to the ingestion of growth hormones, antibiotics, and other substances for the purpose of increasing the output of milk and meat.
- **Exploitation and sacrifice of rabbits.** Between 75 and 90 days after being born, rabbits are sacrificed after having spent their entire lives in captivity.
- **National holidays.** The traditional running of the bulls make a bloody spectacle out of the torture and death of these animals for the amusement of a few.
- **Hunting and fishing.** Daily, millions of animals die of suffocation or after having been shot. Many are returned to the water, injured by hooks or nets, or flee, bleeding from bullet wounds or the bites of hunting dogs.
- **Bee-keeping.** The process of harvesting honey causes the death of masses of bees (either squashed or mutilated), as well as the unjust abuse caused by making them work exhaustively to produce a precious food product that will later be stolen and replaced by a simple mixture of water and sugar.
- **Exploitation of pigs.** Despite being one of the smartest animals in existence, far surpassing dogs, human beings exploit and torture pigs with rare cruelty. The modern pork industry kills millions of pigs every day all over the world after they have endured months of hard conditions.
- **Exploitation of lambs and sheep.** The harvesting of milk, meat, leather, and wool, as well as other derivatives from these species reduces their existence to a brief period of life that is destined for ultimate sacrifice.
- **Exploitation of chickens.** After only 35 days of life, a chicken is ready to be sacrificed. They live a short life, spent stuffed in fattening farms, with their beaks half amputated (without anesthetics) to prevent them from attacking their fellows. For their part, laying chickens spend their lives piled into wire cages. There they spend about two years until their egg production decreases, and they are killed. In its natural habitat, a chicken could grow to be 15– or 20–years old.
- **Testing.** Every year, millions of animals all over the world die as a result of testing. Primates, monkeys, dogs, cats, horses, bovines, pigs, sheep, goats, rabbits, ferrets, chinchillas, groundhogs, possums, armadillos, guinea pigs, hamsters, and an ongoing list of mammals are tortured and sacrificed in labs the world over.

Where do I start?

The first step towards a vegan diet is abandoning the consumption of foods like meat, fish, and eggs. At the beginning, this could be a little complicated and, depending on our will power, might have to be done gradually. Many vegans started by abandoning animal-based products little by little until one fine day they discovered that it had been a long time since they last ate one and that they had already grown used to not having them. By transitioning gradually, we can fortify our eating habits and reinforce our conviction in the fact that we have made the correct choice. Regardless of how the first step towards veganism is taken, it is important to keep in mind a series of key issues:

The basic facts of vegan nutrition. Types of food, nutrition content, how to combine them . . . you don't need to be an expert on the matter, but it is a good idea to consult a specialized book (like the one you have in your hands), flip through health publications that speak on the matter, or subscribe to some kind of informative electronic newsletter about veganism. Familiarize yourself with:

* Where to buy vegan products.

* Simple recipes for daily meals.

* Vegan restaurants and establishments.

* How to change events and celebrations to conform to a type of food.

It can be a little complicated at the start. We can do it progressively, by "vegetizing" the food we are serving: vegetable-based appetizers, vegan paellas or burgers, exotic fruit smoothies, and so on.

Another important step at the time of making the transition to a vegan diet is learning how to naturally change our daily eating habits. One easy way to do this is to ask yourself the following questions:

* **Am I eating too much protein?** The majority of the western population consumes twice as much protein as it needs. Our body is not prepared to store such an amount, and we subject it to extra work in order to process and get rid of it. We can start by eating fewer red meats, cold cuts, and fish and by substituting these progressively with protein-rich foods like soybeans, legumes, tofu, tempeh, cereals, and nuts.

* **Do I eat too much saturated fat?** The consumption of fatty acids is essential for our bodies. However, the proper amount for a balanced diet should be around 30 percent, and we tend to exceed this average, especially by eating saturated fats, which are not recommended and will elevate cholesterol levels. To change this habit, we need to give much more importance to those foods rich in mono-unsaturated fats such as cold-pressed olive oil, nuts, and oleaginous seeds.

* **Do I eat enough fruits and vegetables?** The World Health Organization (WHO) recommends a minimum daily intake of five servings of fruits and vegetables. They are a good source of antioxidants, vitamins, minerals, and fiber that protect and nourish the body. It is important to progressively increase our daily intake as a fundamental step in our transition to a healthier diet.

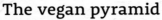

The vegan pyramid

The vegan diet pyramid is divided into the following groups, by order of importance:

Cereals (6 to 11 servings a day): pasta, rice, bread, breakfast cereal, wheat, corn, oats, quinoa, spelt, millet, etc. Example of 1 serving: 1 slice of bread, 30 g (1 oz) of breakfast cereal, 120 g (4 oz) of cooked cereals or pasta, and two tablespoons of wheat germ.

Vegetables and leafy greens (3 or more servings a day): carrots, spinach, cabbage, peppers, celery, tomatoes, chard, potatoes, onions, peas, asparagus, Brussels sprouts, etc. Example of 1 serving: ½ plate of lettuce or similar, 50 g (about 2 oz) of raw vegetables, 80 g (about 3 oz) of cooked vegetables, and one glass of vegetable juice.

Fruits and nuts (2 or more servings a day): oranges, apples, bananas, strawberries, mangoes, avocados, pears, apricots, dried apricots, plums, dried figs, etc. Example of 1 serving: 1 apple, 1 banana, 120 g (4 oz) of sliced fruit, and one glass of fruit juice.

Calcium-rich foods (6 to 8 servings a day): broccoli, spinach, enriched soy milk, tofu, dried figs, almonds, sesame seeds, etc. Example of 1 serving: ½ glass of enriched soy shake, 60 g (about 2 oz) of calcium-enriched tofu (1 slice), ½ glass of calcium-enriched orange juice, 60 g (about 2 oz) of almonds, 240 g (8.5 oz, or one plate) of calcium-rich vegetables (broccoli, cabbage, collard greens), 240 g (8.5 oz) of calcium-rich legumes (soybeans, white beans, etc.), and 5 figs.

Legumes and their derivatives (2 to 3 servings a day): garbanzos, lentils, soy, tempeh, tofu, etc. Example of 1 serving: 1 plate of cooked legumes, 120 g (4 oz) of tofu or tempeh, 3 handfuls of walnuts, and 2 glasses of soy shake.

Others (1 to 2 servings a day): olive oil, vegetable milk, juices, vegetable burgers, vitamin B12-enriched foods (like certain vegetable milks, some soy products, or breakfast cereals).

Let's eat well

The list of vegan ingredients is interminable, but here are, ordered by food group, some of the more common ones that we can use to create any number of tasty, creative, and healthy recipes.

Vegetables and greens

Tasty, healthy, and nutritious, they are among the main components of a vegan diet. Found on the second fundamental level of the food pyramid (surpassed only by cereals), they contain a great deal of nutrients, slow absorbing carbohydrates, and dietetic fiber.

Chard. Rich in fiber and minerals like potassium, magnesium, and iron, as well as vitamins A and C. Has very few calories (28 per every 100 g or 3.5 oz), which makes it ideal for weight loss diets. We can find chard at any time of the year, although the best times are at the end of autumn and the beginning of spring. When choosing, it's best to go for the bunches with bright leaves and no brown spots on the edges or main rib. It has a short shelf life, so it's better to eat 2 or 3 days after it is collected. It is, however, possible to freeze it after scalding it in boiling water for a couple of minutes beforehand. You can eat the leaves boiled or raw, while the main ribs can be used in soups, stews, or casseroles.

Garlic. One of the most-used aromatic ingredients in the kitchen. It is rich in minerals like calcium, iron, and phosphorus, as well as B vitamins. It contains 110 calories in every 100 g or 3.5 oz and is an excellent diuretic and blood tonic. You can find garlic at the market at any time during the year.

Green garlic, or scallions, can be found in the spring and early summer, as well as garlic scapes. When buying dry garlic, it's better to choose heads that are firm to the touch and have no pits on their surface. To keep its flavor from lingering after the meal, you can open them in the middle and remove the sprout inside. Another way to mitigate its intense flavor is to soak it for an hour before cooking.

Artichoke. This green vegetable native to the north of Africa contains an important cache of minerals like iron and calcium, as well as vitamins A, B, and C. It only has 38 calories per every 100 g or 3.5 oz, and it's ideal for incorporating into weight loss diets. You can find it in markets between the months of October and June. When you pick it out, it should be hard to the touch, compact, and with leaves that are a clear and bright shade of green. One simple trick for picking them out is to squeeze the artichoke next to your ear: if you hear a crunch, it means that it's fresh. It keeps best when stored inside a closed plastic bag and placed in the refrigerator. To keep it from drying out before it's time to use, it's better not to cut the stalk until you are going to cook it. You can eat it raw, steamed, boiled, fried, battered, grilled, or baked.

Celery. Rich in minerals like potassium, sodium, and phosphorus, it has a good amount of fiber and vitamins A and C. It's one of the vegetables with the least amount of calories (only 12 for every 100 g or 3.5 oz) and can be found at the market all year long. When choosing, opt for ones that are firm, compact, and of a clear green color. Discard any that have blotches or dry spots. To keep it longer, put it in the refrigerator's crisper drawer wrapped in damp paper towels. You can eat it boiled in all kinds of soups and stews, raw and cut in strips, or grated as a tasty complement for any kind of salad.

Eggplant. Originating from India, it is available during the whole year. It's rich in calcium, potassium, and vitamins A, B, and C. Choose those that have tight, shiny skin. One good trick for picking one is to check how fresh

the tip of the stalk is, which will indicate how much time has passed since it was collected. You can eat it stewed, stuffed, baked, battered, fried, grilled, boiled, steamed, and in creams or purees.

Broccoli. This vegetable belongs to the cabbage family and is very rich in fiber and minerals like sulfur, iron, and calcium. In fact, it is considered to be one of the green vegetables with the most nutrients. The best time to pick it out is between the months of October and April, and before you buy it, look for bunches that display a firm surface and dark green color. The best way to take advantage of all its qualities is to steam or boil it for just 3 minutes.

Zucchini. Rich in fiber and minerals (potassium and calcium), the best time to get it is during warmer months, although it is available year round. When picking out zucchini, it is best to skip the bigger specimens since they will contain a greater amount of seeds and their meat will be less tender. You can eat this raw as well as cooked, and it allows for a multitude of culinary preparations.

Squash. Rich in calcium, iron, and zinc, as well as vitamins A, B, and C. It only has 12 calories for every 100 g or 3.5 oz. You can choose from two varieties: summer squash (with clear, thin skin), and winter squash (a bit sweeter but with less water). Butternut squash (a kind of winter squash) may be used in sweet recipes.

Onion. Available year-round from the market, although the best time to get it is during the months of spring. Rich in minerals like potassium, phosphorus, magnesium, and calcium. It can be eaten raw as well as cooked in all kinds of recipes. It is an ideal ingredient for salads, for which the sweeter varieties are best suited. To avoid tearing up while cutting this vegetable, hold it briefly under cold running water once it has been peeled. The sting that causes your eyes to water is caused by its release of a volatile acid full of sulfur compounds.

Cabbage. Available in a wide variety, some of the most common are wavy or smooth-leafed cabbage, red cabbage, collard greens, Brussels sprouts, or Napa cabbage. They are all available from markets year round.

Asparagus. Originating from the Mediterranean basin, there are two main varieties: white asparagus and green asparagus. The first grows underground and because of this, does not develop chlorophyll, which gives its distinct lack of color. Green, or wild, asparagus is sought after for its intense flavor. Although both are available year-round thanks to winter crops, their best time runs between the months of April and May. When picking them out, be sure to look for the ones that have tightly closed and compact tips, as well as a straight and firm stalk.

Spinach. This vegetable from Asia Minor is rich in iron as well as vitamins A, B, and C. It's available year-round in its different varieties according to the look and size of its leaves (smooth, curly, large, or small). When purchasing, look for the bunches with uniform leaves that are a clear and bright shade of green. It can be stored in the fridge for at least a couple of weeks. Nevertheless, it's better to keep it in a perforated plastic bag so the leaves stay fresher longer.

Cucumber. Even though you can find it in the market year-round, the best time for eating it is between the spring and autumn months. It has very few calories (only 12 in every 100 g or 3.5 oz) and is rich in nutrients like iron, potassium, and vitamin C.

Peppers. You can differentiate between two large varieties of fresh peppers: the sweet ones and the spicy ones. In the first group, you will find multi-colored peppers that are best bought during the summer and the beginning of autumn, although they are available year-round. As far as spicy peppers are concerned, jalapeno, serrano, and poblano peppers stand out the most.

Leeks. Rich in fiber and minerals like iron and calcium, these contain a considerable amount of vitamins A and C. They are available year-round. When choosing, opt for ones that are smaller, with green, shiny leaves, and a firm white stalk.

Radish. Available year-round, but those found during the spring (their natural season) are tastier. They contain nutrients like phosphorus, calcium, iron, as well as vitamins B and C.

Beets. These can be found in markets year-round and are rich in sugar, fiber, and nutrients like potassium, sodium, and calcium.

Tomatoes. An excellent source of fiber, as well as potassium, phosphorus, and vitamins C and E. There are nearly 100 varieties of tomatoes that we can classify according to size, shape, or use. Generally, you can distinguish between two large categories:

> **Salad tomatoes**. In this group, you will find beefsteak (very full and meaty), heirloom varieties like montserrat (lobe-shaped and quite empty, but tasty), and cherry tomatoes (small, with an intense red color).

> **Cooking tomatoes**. The most notable are the Daniela (spherical and juicy), and pear or roma varieties (ideal for making conserves and sauces).

Carrots. This vegetable is rich in vitamin A, as well as calcium, potassium, and phosphorus. It is available year-round, but the smaller and thinner ones found during spring are tastier.

Legumes

A basic source of protein and carbohydrates, eating legumes regularly will grant health benefits and help with the prevention of illnesses. Their protein content can surpass that of meat, especially when it comes to dry legumes.

Common bean. These receive different names according to their country of origin (beans, white beans, French beans, etc.). This legume is very rich in fiber, potassium, and iron, although its main components are carbohydrates. It also has a good amount of vegetable protein. Its ability to absorb the flavor of the ingredients it accompanies makes it ideal for making all types of vegetable stews and soups. Mind you, before cooking these, it is best to rehydrate them by submerging them in cold water for approximately 12 hours. Depending on the variety, cooking time will vary between 1 and 3 hours (this time will be reduced if using a pressure cooker). You can also opt for precooked and dehydrated beans that will only take 30 minutes to cook. Among the different varieties of this dry legume, white beans, red beans, kidney beans, and black-eyed peas are some that stand out.

Peas. Originating from the Middle East and Central Asia, the best time to eat these fresh is between the months of March and May. If they are dry, you can find them year-round. They are rich in B vitamins as well as calcium, iron, and potassium. They contain 78 calories for every 100 g or 3.5 oz.

Broad bean. Fresh broad beans are rich in nutrients like vitamins B and C, calcium, and phosphorus. They are available in markets from the end of winter to the beginnings of spring.

Soybean. Originating from China, this is one of the legumes richest in good quality protein, surpassing even the amounts found in meats. It is also rich in fiber, carbohydrates, and fats that are, for the most part, polyunsaturated. It has a high amount of minerals like calcium, iron, magnesium, potassium, and phosphorus, as well as vitamins B and E. Among the most common varieties of this legume are the red soybean or adzuki bean, green soybean or mung bean, and yellow soybean (used the most in the kitchen). Soy is a very versatile food from which you may obtain a great variety of products: flour, oil, lecithin, soy drink, tofu, tamari, and tempeh.

Garbanzo. A very carbohydrate-rich legume with a higher amount of protein than the rest of its peers. It is also rich in fiber, calcium, iron, potassium, and magnesium. Unlike the rest of the legumes, when it comes time to cook dry garbanzos, you should start with lukewarm water, not cold, to keep them from hardening. You can also buy them already cooked, toasted, canned, or jarred. Once cooked, they will keep well for a few days in a hermetically-sealed container in the refrigerator.

Lentils. Originating from southeast Asia, this legume is rich in carbohydrates, iron, and vitamin B, although they have less fiber than the rest of the legumes. Their low fat content makes them ideal for regulating the levels of blood cholesterol. It is not necessary to rehydrate lentils before cooking them, you just need to cover them with cold water for a few minutes beforehand to keep the skin from drying out and falling off. You can find dry lentils in jars or in bulk. In any case, you should make sure they are whole and give off a fresh odor, with a light aroma of walnuts. Among the most common varieties, you will find Spanish Pardina lentils (small and brown-colored), yellow lentils, red lentils (salmon-colored), and du Puy lentils (very tasty).

Spices

Originating mostly from Asia, using them lends aroma and flavor to all kinds of culinary preparations.

Saffron. Used to give aroma and color to several culinary preparations like paellas, sauces, stews, and soups.

Cinnamon. Available in sticks, powder, or extract. Very common in the making of all kinds of desserts.

Cardamom. This spice originates from India and has an intense, citric flavor.

Clove. This is one of the most aromatic spices out there. It is used whole or ground and always in small quantities as its aroma and flavor are very intense.

Ginger. This spice's citric flavor brings interesting contrast to different culinary preparations.

Nutmeg. Spicy and sweet, with a lightly citric and very aromatic flavor, this spice is grated at the precise time when it is needed, although you may also find it in powdered form.

Paprika. Powdered spice obtained from grinding specific dried, red peppers. It can be sweet or spicy.

Pepper. Originating from India, there is a great variety of pepper, but the most common are black pepper, white pepper, and green pepper.

Vanilla. One of the most intense aromatics used in gastronomy. It may be found in powder or liquid and is often used for making all kinds of desserts.

Fruits

Tasty, healthy, and rich in nutrients, fruits are found on the second level of the food pyramid and are the ideal complement for a vegan diet. They contain few calories and have a high percentage of water (between 80 and 95 percent), carbohydrates, sugar, and antioxidant substances (vitamin C, vitamin E, beta-carotene, lycopene, lutein, flavonoids, anthocyanins, etc.).

Avocado. Originating from Mexico, Colombia, and Venezuela, it is very rich in fats and high in calories (135 calories per 100 g or 3.5 oz). Among the most common varieties are Bacon (available starting from October), Fuerte (available year round), and Pinkerton (between the months of February and March).

Apricot. A firm, juicy fruit with a delicious sweet flavor. The best time for these is between the months of May and September. They are noted for their elevated amounts of fiber and provitamin A, an antioxidant. They should be purchased when well-ripened to best enjoy their aroma and sweetness.

Blueberries. This fruit from Europe and Asia grows wildly on the edges of paths and gullies. They ripen during the months of summer and autumn and can be found year-round, thanks to winter farming. The most common blueberry varieties are the black, or American blueberry, and the tart, or red, blueberry.

Cherries. A summer fruit that can be enjoyed from the end of April to mid August. Its color can vary between a reddish yellow, to an intense red, almost black. When purchasing, it is best to choose those that are meatier, with a firm, shiny, and whole skin. Generally, the larger the cherry, the tastier it is. Cherries are noted for their elevated amount of calories and, above all, fructose, although they have fewer calories than other fruits. They also contain a significant amount of fiber.

Plums. Depending on the color, we can distinguish between the yellow (sour and juicy), red (sweeter than the yellow), black (the best for cooking), and greengage varieties (very sought after for its sweet flavor). They all begin appearing in markets during the hotter months.

Coconut. When picking these out, its better to choose ones that have a lot of water inside. To check, all you need to do is shake it and listen for the sloshing of the water. Once opened, it should be eaten the same day or stored in pieces in a container full of water for a maximum of four days. This fruit is full of calories, reaching as high as 351 for every 100 g or 3.5 oz.

Strawberries. Low-calorie fruits rich in carbohydrates, fiber, and vitamin C. They belong to the group of red fruits in which you will also find sloe, blackberries, redcurrant, and blueberries.

Figs. Originating from the Mediterranean basin, there are several varieties distinguished by the color of their skin (white, blue, dark red, etc.). Rich in carbohydrates and fiber, as well as potassium, calcium, and magnesium. When buying, look for ones with a good consistency and soft texture that give lightly when pressed by your fingers (a sign that they are nice and ripe). This is a very delicate fruit that can be kept for no more than three days in the fridge.

Kiwi. This fruit originates from some regions in the Himalayas, and the best time to get them starts in October and runs until May, although the New Zealand variety can be consumed from the end of May until the beginning of November. They have a high content of vitamin C that can be twice as high as in oranges. When purchasing, look for ones that are intact and free of blotches.

Limes. This refreshing citrus is available year-round and is one of the fruits with the least amount of calories (only 6 calories for every 100 g or 3.6 oz). It is rich in potassium and vitamin C, and may vary in sourness depending

on the variety. You should pick out ones that have shinier skin with an intense shade of green.

Lemon. Similar to the lime, this citrus fruit is very rich in vitamin C (45 mg for every 100 g, or 3.5 oz) and potassium. Available year-round, always buy ones with shiny, smooth skin and small pores.

Tangerine. Originating from China, it has vitamins A and C, as well as calcium and magnesium. The most common varieties are clementine (sweet flesh and very aromatic juice) and clemenvilla (thin-skinned and smooth, so much so that it can be hard to peel at times). They can be found in markets between the months of September and March. Similarly to all citrus fruits, you should choose the heaviest ones, a sure sign that they are succulent and full of juice.

Mango. Originating from India, this tasty and aromatic fruit is found year-round in markets. There are several varieties that differ in the color of their skin: green, orange, red, yellow, pink, and even violet. It has a good amount of calories (60 calories for every 100 g or 3.5 oz) and is very rich in vitamins A and C, as well as in potassium and magnesium.

Apple. It is an excellent source of vitamin C and fiber, and it's also rich in calcium, phosphorus, potassium, and iron. Among the most common varieties you will find the Granny Smith (green-colored and slightly sour), Golden Delicious (greenish yellow and crunchy), McIntosh (red and tart), and the Fuji (yellow-red color, very aromatic and juicy). Most of them can be found from September until June, although some may be available year-round.

Peach. Fruit of Chinese origin that appears in markets at the end of May. It is very rich in sugars and mineral salts like potassium. You should look for ones that have smooth, spotless skin and no bruises on the surface, since they tend to rot easily. Among the different varieties you'll find the nectarine (similar to the peach but with smooth, thin, shiny skin) and the Saturn peach (with a flattened appearance and a very aromatic pulp).

Melons. Their exterior can be green, yellow, or orange, depending on the variety (canary, cantaloupe, galia, etc.). They are summer fruits and the best time to eat them is during the hottest months of the year. They are rich in fiber, potassium, and vitamins A, B, and C. When purchasing, check for ripeness by pressing on the end opposite the stalk, which should be soft to the touch.

Orange. There are two major groups of oranges: sweet and sour. The first is the most often used in gastronomy and consists of the navel, Valencia, and blood varieties. You can enjoy this citrus fruit during all months of the year. Nutritionally speaking, they are noted for their high content of vitamin C, folic acid, and minerals such as potassium, calcium, and magnesium. A large part of this fruit's aroma is concentrated in the skin, for which reason many recipes, especially desserts, call for grating it.

Loquat. This fruit appears in markets starting in April and their season ends in June. It has a high sugar content and is rich in fiber and minerals like calcium and magnesium.

Pears. Originating from eastern Europe and western Asia, the most common varieties found in markets are the Bartlett (sweet, with a mottled skin), Bosc (with a grainy pulp), and the D'Anjou (with a smooth, green skin). All are noted for their high content of sugar, fiber, and minerals like potassium.

Pineapple. This fruit originates from South America, specifically from Brazil. It is rich in vitamins A, B, and C, as well as fiber, potassium, and calcium. It is available in markets during all months of the year. Before purchasing, you should make sure the skin of the fruit does not sink under pressure from your finger. Once it is cut, it should be eaten as soon as possible, since it will quickly deteriorate.

Bananas. Originating from southern Asia, this sweet and aromatic fruit is rich in carbohydrates, potassium, magnesium. It is available year-round and when purchasing, look for ones that are not battered or bruised, since they can deteriorate with ease. To avoid darkening the skin, it's best not to store them in the refrigerator.

Grapefruit. The best time to get this citrus fruit related to oranges, tangerines, and lemons is between the months of October and March. It is rich in vitamin C and minerals like potassium, phosphorus, and magnesium. The most common varieties are yellow grapefruits (with a bitter-sour taste), and red grapefruits (sweeter).

Watermelon. Originating from tropical African countries, there are more than 50 varieties that differ among shape, weight, and color. It is full of vitamins A and C, potassium, magnesium, and fiber. It appears in markets starting in May, although the ideal time is between July and September. Its thick skin will let you keep it at room temperature without fear of it spoiling. This is much better anyway, since excessive cold can ruin it.

Grapes. A fleshy fruit rich in sugars and with a higher calorie content. Available in markets starting in June, give the cluster a shake before purchasing to make sure all the grapes stick to their spots. Once you get them home, grapes will keep for a long time if kept in the fridge, up to 15 days. To fully enjoy their flavor, it is best to take them out of the fridge an hour before eating.

Nuts

Tasty, nutritious, and full of energy, these are one of the main staples of a vegan diet. Their elevated amounts of minerals, high quality proteins, and fats surpass most vegetables and their nutritional worth is first-class. In addition to that, they can combined with an infinite number of culinary preparations, such as salads, soups, creams, stews, sauces, and desserts.

Almonds. These are one of the nuts richest in fiber as well as unsaturated fats (beneficial for cardiovascular health). You can eat them raw, toasted, or fried. Almond milk is also a very nutritious and healthy food.

Cashews. Originating from the Amazon basin, this tasty nut is rich in fatty acids and minerals like selenium (a very effective antioxidant) and magnesium.

Hazelnuts. One of the most energy-packed nuts thanks to their high calorie content (566 for every 100 g, or 3.5 oz), they are rich in fatty acids and minerals like iron, calcium, and potassium. They are also known for their vitamin E content, a nutrient that helps prevent degenerative illnesses.

Peanuts. One of the nuts with the most protein, folic acid, and vitamin E.

Chestnuts. If you are looking to maintain your waistline, this nut is perfect thanks to its lower caloric content (165 for every 100 g, or 3.5 oz). However, it does have a higher amount of complex carbohydrates, important to keep in mind for those with diabetes.

Dates. One of the most calorie-rich dry fruits available (227 calories for every 100 g, or 3.5 oz), it is also rich in sugars, potassium, iron, and magnesium.

Dry figs. Excellent source of potassium, calcium, and iron. They are squashed-looking and a violet-gray color, or mottled, with a yellowish pulp and a viscous consistency.

Walnuts. Very nutritious and calorie-rich, this nut is highly recommended for people who require lots of extra energy (athletes, students, people who are recovering, and so on).

Pine nuts. Rich in high quality proteins and fiber, this nut may be eaten raw or toasted. It is recommended for people who are suffering from deficiencies.

Pistachios. One of the most energy-packed nuts, with 630 calories for every 100 g, or 3.5 oz, and rich in vitamin A and folic acid.

Raisins. A very nutritious dry fruit. Among the most common varieties you will find the Corinthe raisin (made from black grapes) and the Sultana (made from white grapes).

Sprouts

Thanks to their rich cache of vitamins and minerals, germinates are an excellent source of nutrients. They stimulate the digestive system and contain a good amount of antioxidants (vitamin C, beta-Carotene), barely have any calories, and are cheap. You can add them to salads, sauces, and stir-fries.

Alfalfa. Possibly one of the most nutritious and complete foods you can find. Rich in protein, carbohydrates, polyunsaturated fats, and fiber, as well as vitamins A, C, E, and minerals such as potassium, magnesium, calcium, and iron.

Adzuki. The sprouts from this nutritious bean contain all the essential amino acids, iron, and vitamin C.

Broccoli. These sprouts are rich in vitamins A, B, C, E, and mineral salts like potassium, calcium, iodine, magnesium, and sulfur. Recommended to eat during menopause, because it acts as phytoestrogen, while supplying calcium.

Lentils. Sprout rich in carbohydrates, protein, fiber, iron, calcium, phosphorus, potassium, and vitamins A, B, C, and E. Helps regulate the levels of blood sugar and reduce cholesterol.

Leeks. These sprouts are rich in vitamins A, B, C, E, and in minerals such as calcium, phosphorus, iron, sulfur, and magnesium. They reduce cholesterol and boost the immune system.

Radish. Rich in vitamins A and B, as well as iron, potassium, calcium, magnesium, sodium, and phosphorus.

Soybean. Refreshing, tender, and tasty, soybean sprouts contain a good amount of protein and vitamins.

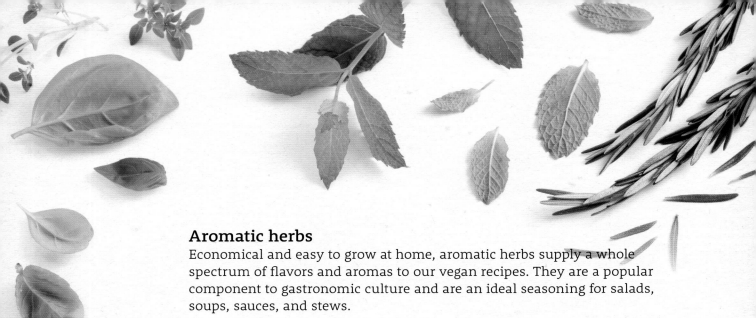

Aromatic herbs

Economical and easy to grow at home, aromatic herbs supply a whole spectrum of flavors and aromas to our vegan recipes. They are a popular component to gastronomic culture and are an ideal seasoning for salads, soups, sauces, and stews.

Basil. Its leaves, fresh as well as dry, can be added to any pasta-based dish, vegetables, and legumes. It can be stored dry for months in a well-sealed jar, or fresh for a few days in the fridge.

Cilantro. Also known as coriander, it is very similar to parsley, but with a much stronger flavor. When cooking, we also use its ground seeds to add aroma to dishes.

Dill. Similar in flavor to fennel and anise, it is best to use it fresh, since it will lose a large portion of its aroma when dried. Keep in mind to be careful with the amount you add because it can overpower the taste of other ingredients.

Tarragon. Its leaves (fresh or dry) are sweet and tart and used in the making of all kinds of sauces, salads, and adobos.

Fennel. From this aromatic herb, we can use the bulb (chopped in salads and soups) and the leaves (as an aromatic in stews) by taking advantage of its characteristic anise-like odor.

Bay. Fresh or dried bay leaves may be used to add flavor and aroma to all kinds of soups, sauces, and stews.

Mint. The intense chlorophyll odor from its leaves makes it ideal for adding aroma to a great variety of recipes.

Oregano. With a slightly tart taste, this herb is typical to Italian cuisine and adds aroma and flavor to many dishes.

Parsley. One of the most popular aromatics, it is used often as a garnish for all kinds of dishes. Keep in mind that the stalk of this plant contains much more flavor and aroma than its leaves.

Chervil. It has a sweet and subtle flavor, and is used often as a condiment in French cooking to add aroma to soups, sauces, and salads.

Rosemary. Better to use it dry, as it is slightly bitter when fresh. It is ideal for use in rices.

Sage. Another of the aromatic herbs typical to Italian cuisine. Unlike rosemary, it is better to use the leaves fresh in order to take advantage of the intensity of its aroma and flavor.

Thyme. Its leaves supply an intense and slightly acrid flavor to soups, stews, and sauces.

Cereals

Found in powders, flakes, flours, semolina, and pastas, cereals occupy the base of the vegan nutritional food pyramid. They supply a great amount of both fast-absorbing (after ingesting, they are absorbed quickly into the blood) and slow-absorbing (in the form of fiber) carbohydrates. When combined with legumes, they supply biologically valuable protein, and in this sense, are excellent meat substitutes. They are also rich in minerals like calcium, phosphorus, iron, and potassium. They contain all forms of vitamin B, as well as vitamin E.

Rice. Rich in carbohydrates and protein, it contains no gluten and can be obtained in an unending number of varieties (short-grain white, brown, parboiled, round grain, glutinous, aromatic, etc.).

Buckwheat. One of the most energy-packed and nutritious cereals. Does not contain gluten and can be purchased in grain, flakes, or flour.

Oats. Usually eaten in flakes or as a drink. One of the most protein, fat, and carbohydrate rich cereals. It is also quite full of calories (335 calories for every 100 g or 3.5 oz).

Barley. Can be obtained in grains, flakes, or as a drink. Its elevated content of a type of soluble fiber (beta-glucan) is an excellent ally against LDL cholesterol (bad cholesterol).

Rye. Rich in fiber, iron, and group E vitamins, it is used often for making breads.

Corn. Rich in carbohydrates, vitamin B, and fiber. It lacks gluten and can be obtained fresh as kernels or cobs, or dry as flour or semolina.

Millet. Rich in vitamin A, iron, and phosphorus, it is available in grains or in flakes.

Quinoa. It tastes similar to brown rice, and is rich in carbohydrates and fiber. It does not contain gluten and is very rich in high quality protein.

Wheat. It is made up of 10 percent protein, and is rich in minerals such as selenium, magnesium, iron, and copper, as well as in group B vitamins. This grain can be used to make other products such as couscous, bulgur, or seitan (wheat protein).

Salty seasonings and condiments

These bring the final touch of flavor and aroma to a multitude of recipes. A fundamental part of any pantry, they enrich and season all kinds of dishes.

Oil. Among the vegetable oils, olive oil is the most recommended for its health properties. It is rich in unsaturated fats and contains vitamins A and E. Other healthy vegetable oils are sunflower, soybean, sesame, or corn oil.

Capers. Rich in unsaturated fats and low in calories, these are a very healthy condiment to add to any salty dish.

Seaweed. Wakame, dulse, kombu, nori, agar agar . . . there are innumerable types of delicious and healthy seaweed that we can use to accompany dishes made with cereals, vegetables, salads, soups, or legumes.

Umeboshi plum. This fermented plum, often used in Chinese and Japanese kitchens, contains twice as much protein and minerals than other fruits. It can be purchased whole, in glass jars, or in bulk in natural food markets. You can eat it by itself or diced in soups and salads.

Gomashio. This nutritious condiment is made from sesame seeds and sea salt. It is rich in minerals, unsaturated fatty cardio-soluble acids, lecithin, vitamins, and proteins. It can be easily made at home by combining 1 tablespoon of salt for every 10–15 tablespoons of sesame seeds that have been previously toasted in a skillet.

Miso. This is a very aromatic paste made by fermenting soybeans with sea salt. It is used as a condiment for salads and rices.

Salt. Available in different shapes, textures, and flavors, salt is rich in minerals. It is important to limit how much is eaten, especially in the case of those suffering from hypertension or cardiovascular illnesses.

Soy sauce. Used often in Chinese and Japanese cooking, it is created via the lactic acid fermentation of the seeds of the plant that goes by the same name. It is a salty condiment, but at the same time it adds a touch of sweetness to dishes.

Vinegar. One of the most used ingredients in the kitchen, it brings recipes an extra amount of key taste and aroma. You can find it in many varieties: white vinegar, wine vinegar, cider vinegar, rice vinegar, and others.

Wasabi. A very tasty and spicy cream made from Japanese radishes.

Sweet seasonings and condiments

Sugar. It is best to opt for raw sugar or brown sugar, both made from sugar cane. This first has fewer calories than white sugar, and is rich in vitamins and minerals. Whole cane sugar or Sucanat, for its own part, retains all of its nutritional properties as it has not been refined.

Vegetable milk. Made from rice, soybean, oats, or almonds, they contain no lactose and have a great variety of nutrients (protein, carbohydrates, minerals, and vitamins). You can use these types of drinks in the same culinary ways that you would use cow's milk. Following that, you could use them to make all kinds of desserts, sauces, creams, soups, and shakes. Once open, they need to be refrigerated and should always be consumed no more than 3 or 4 days later.

Agave syrup. A healthy alternative to sugar, this is a type of vegetable juice extracted from a species of cactus native to the tropical Americas and the Caribbean. This syrup has twice the sweetening power of sugar thanks to its high fructose content.

Maple syrup. Made using the sap from maple trees, which are native to Canada and the United States. It has a considerable sweetening ability, and is rich in minerals (potassium and magnesium, especially) and vitamin E.

Others

Wheat germ. Its very high concentration of vitamin E makes it a great antioxidant perfect for for ailing people, or those suffering from bodily fatigue. It can be obtained in flakes or granulated and is a good accompaniment for cereals.

Brewer's and nutritional yeasts. This first-class, energy-packed food has a high protein content and is a valuable complement in the vegan diet. It is highly recommended for adolescents because of its minerals, like zinc.

Seitan. Made from wheat gluten, it is very rich in protein, making it a fundamental culinary addition to the vegan diet. Its calorie content is very low and it usually looks like a dark brown-colored ball with a firm, but very malleable, texture. You can cook it just like you would meat: grilled, battered, roasted, stewed, or as filling.

Tofu. Soy milk curd is an excellent substitute for meat, thanks to its high protein content. It can be used for different dishes like tofu burgers, or as an accompaniment for salads or vegetables.

Tempeh. Made by fermenting granulated soy and used to accompany salads or as an ingredient in all kinds of soups, creams, stews, and pastas.

Animal-based ingredients

Those who follow a strictly vegan diet know how hard it can be to avoid animal-based ingredients that seem to be present in an infinite number of foods. Legislation compels the food industry to specify all the components of their products on the label. Additives, dyes, preservatives, the terminology that is used is complex and most of the words sound like gibberish. So here is a brief glossary that will help you spot the most common and used animal-based ingredients in the processed food industry:

- **Carminic acid (E120).** Pigment obtained from the cochineal that is used as a dye in food and drinks.
- **Oleic acid.** Liquid obtained when pressing animal fat. It is used for making margarine.
- **Lactic acid (E270).** Acid produced by fermenting sugar in milk. Found in candy products, carbonated beverages, and sauces.
- **Albumin.** Substance found in egg whites that is used as an agglutinant in food.
- **Isinglass.** A gelatinous substance obtained from the gills of certain fish that is used to clarify carbonated beverages, jellies, etc.
- **Gelatin.** Extracted from different animal tissues, it is used for making candy, cookies, and gelatin pastes.
- **Glycerin.** Transparent and colorless liquid that may be derived from animal fat. Used as a moisturizer to improve the texture and flavor of some processed foods.
- **Calcium mesoinositol hexaphosphate.** Found in baked products, carbonated drinks, and processed vegetables.
- **Disodium inosinate.** Used to improve the flavor of certain foods.
- **Lactose.** A flavor agent used as a sweetener.
- **Lecithin.** Fatty, animal-based substance that is used as an emulsifier in baked products and candy.
- **Whey.** Extracted from milk after having removed the casein and most of the fat. Found in margarine, cookies, and snacks.

A well-equipped kitchen

A vegan kitchen is simple to prep, but it requires certain tools to make the job quicker and more comfortable. The use of certain knives is particularly valuable since many recipes call for peeling, cutting, chopping, crushing, or grating all kinds of vegetables, leafy greens, and fruits. These are some of the methods that will be used the most in the kitchen, so it is important to invest in good quality knives, graters, and scissors.

Kitchen scale. Many of the amounts specified in the recipes in this book require the use of a kitchen scale to accurately obtain the amounts called for by the text. When making desserts, it is especially important to accurately measure out ingredients to the specified amounts.

Whisk beater. This practical tool can be electric or powered by hand. It is ideal for whipping egg yolks or whites to form stiff peaks, whipping cream, and emulsifying liquids.

Salad spinner. Tool for making salads with completely dry and crunchy leaves. Also used to quickly dry other leaf vegetables. You can choose among different models, designs, and accessories (electric spinners, handle spinners). Using them will guarantee that your leaf vegetables are perfectly clean.

Steamer basket. These can be made of metal or bamboo and are used to steam vegetables without the ingredients coming into contact with the water. This way, your ingredients will be crunchier and retain a lot more of their nutrients.

Strainer. There are different kinds:

Chinese. A cone-shaped strainer that is used to sift, spread, and strain soups, creams, and sauces. Its curious name comes from the visual likeness it has to an ancient oriental hat.

Long-handled. Available in different sizes, they are usually half-moon shaped and are used to sift ingredients like flour and sugar, blanch vegetables, and remove solids from a broth by using a fine or thick wire mesh.

Colander. Through a series of practical holes at the base of this receptacle, food can be drained of any water (generally after being cooked).

Knives

These are the vegan cook's greatest ally. It is of the utmost importance to be able to count on a good set of knives (high quality, if possible). For peeling, dicing, chopping, and mincing, you can start with a basic collection and continue expanding according to your needs:

Chef's. The blade is approximately 20–25 cm (8–10 in) long, it is wide at the base and narrow at the tip. It gets its name from the fact that most professional cooks consider this knife to be an indispensable element in any kitchen that takes pride in itself. The light curve of the blade allows for efficient and rhythmic movements on the cutting surface.

Utility. The blade measures between 11 and 20 cm (about 4 and 8 in) long. It is best used for peeling fruit and cutting vegetables and leafy greens into pieces.

Serrated. The blade is jagged, long, and straight, measuring between 20 and 30 cm (8 and 12 in). It allows for easy cutting of hard surfaces, for example, the skin of citrus fruits.

Mezzaluna. This knife has a curved blade in a half moon shape that makes it ideal for chopping aromatic herbs and nuts. There are two varieties:

> **Mezzaluna with two handles.** You rock it back and forth on top of the food you are cutting.

> **Mezzaluna with one central handle.** It pairs with a semi-spherical wooden bowl, the curvature of which matches the shape of the blade.

Tomato knife. It has a serrated blade measuring between 11 and 13 cm (about 4 and 5 in) long, which allows it to cleanly cut the skin and pulp of ripe tomatoes without the risk of tearing them up. Some types include a fork-shaped tip that can be used to pierce the thinnest and most delicate slices without splitting them.

Paring. A small knife with a blade measuring between 7 and 10 cm (about 3 and 4 in). Used for peeling, coring, and cutting up small ingredients. Its narrow tip makes it ideal for meticulous work, such as decoratively cutting vegetables, fruits, and leafy greens.

Peeler. It has an opening in the center that allows you to take off the skin from all kinds of root vegetables (carrots, potatoes, etc.) and peel citrus fruits.

Bird's beak paring knife. It has a short (between 5 and 7 cm, or 2 and 3 in), curved blade that resembles the shape of a bird's beak. It makes it easy to cleanly and obliquely cut vegetables.

Bowls. One of the most used elements in the kitchen, this is a very versatile tool that can be made using different materials, according to its intended use.

Glass. Easy to clean, and it allows you to see how your ingredients are mixing inside. Can be put in the freezer, the microwave, and the dishwasher. It is better to acquire tempered glass models, because they can stand more extreme hot and cold temperatures.

Ceramic. This material makes it so that the ingredients in the bowl change temperature slowly, so that they retain heat or cold for a longer period of time.

Melamine. Easy to clean, lightweight, and does not react with acidic elements.

Stainless steel. Unlike other metal materials (like copper or aluminum), these types of bowls do not react with acids and are lighter and more durable than ceramic or glass ones.

Wooden. The least commonly found in the kitchen, it is best not to put these in the dishwasher or leave liquids in them for a long time.

Lemon squeezer. When making different vegan dishes, it is often necessary to use the juice of citrus fruits, such as oranges and lemons. This tool takes up very little space in the kitchen and will let you manually extract the fruits' juice.

Measuring jug. Made from transparent glass and imprinted on the surface with a series of measurements in milliliters, ounces, cups, and grams.

Mortar and pestle. This is a durable container that is used to mash, grind, and mix spices, seeds, and nuts.

Food mill. Made from stainless steel, this is ideal for making all kinds of purees out of vegetables, legumes, and fruit. It is also an excellent tool when making sauces and soups.

Pots/Pans. Generally, it is advisable to have three different sizes: one deep and wide pot or pan for cooking all kinds of vegetables, broths, legumes, and pastas; a medium one; and a small one for sauces. They can be:

Stainless steel. Solid and easy to clean. This is a very durable material that can be cleaned in the dishwasher.

Aluminum and steel. Aluminum is a lightweight material and an excellent conductor, but it reacts badly with the acid present in food. To avoid this, the inside of the pot is covered in a coat of stainless steel.

Copper. This material is an excellent conductor that will let you heat and cool food rapidly.

Cast iron. Plain or enameled, it heats slowly, retains its heat very well, and distributes it evenly.

Clay. They are actually made from fired ceramic and are usually used for making slow-cooked or baked stews.

Grater. Flat or box-shaped, they have different-sized gaps for grating all kinds of vegetables, leafy greens, or fruits.

Skillets. It is best to pick out skillets made from stainless steel or aluminum with a nonstick coating to keep from from clinging to them. You should have two or three different-sized skillets (between 25 and 35 cm, or 10 and 14 in, in diameter).

Cutting board. Can be made of wood or plastic. It is better to get ones with a small groove to collect leftover liquids and juices during the cutting process.

Kitchen shears. For cutting fresh herbs, small stalks, and pieces of fruit. The stainless steel ones are better as they are more durable.

Small, essential electric appliances

There are a number of basic appliances used for making all kinds of vegan dishes. They are electric and some can be pretty bulky, but it's worth it to invest in them if you want to be able to prepare everything much more quickly and comfortably:

- **Mixer.** Stand mixer or hand-held mixer, this is a very practical electrical appliance when you need to beat, mix, or knead soft foods.

- **Juicer.** An interesting tool for making all kinds of fruit and vegetable juices. Try making your own vegan cocktails!

- **Blender.** Indispensable when making soups, sauces, juices, and shakes. There is a huge number of models with different speeds and capacities.

- **Slow cooker.** Small electric appliance that allows for the application of a constant temperature over long periods of time. Capacities can vary between 1 and 7 liters, or a similar amount of quarts.

- **All-in-one kitchen appliance.** These are somewhat ostentatious and can be intrusive in kitchens that do not have a lot of extra room to spare. But it's worth it to learn about these appliances capable of carrying out all sorts of functions like cutting, mixing, kneading, slow cooking, boiling, and steaming. Thermomix is one of the most popular models and there are a multitude of books filled with recipes written to be made with this famous appliance. For more information, log on to http://thermomix.vorwerk.com

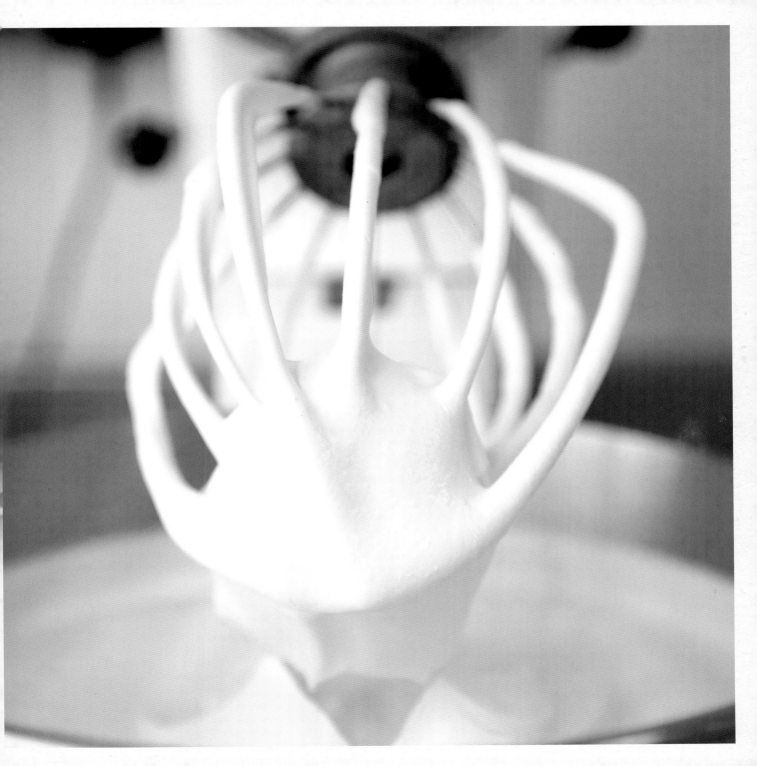

Culinary techniques

When cooking vegan food, it is especially important to use techniques that best preserve the nutritional richness found in the ingredients being used. You can distinguish among the following techniques, depending on which medium is being used for the cooking:

Dry heat cooking

Grilling. The secret to this technique lies in the fire. When grilling, you must control the intensity of the flame if you want to avoid drying out or burning the food. The kind of grill you use will depend on the desired flavor of the grilled food, so whether it is electric, gas, wood, or charcoal.

Broiling. Broiling food is a way to cook ingredients using a very high and even amount of heat. This way, the ingredients will brown nicely on the outside, but remain juicy on the inside. It is a quick way of cooking food that does not require oil or fat, which makes it quite healthy. You can broil tempeh, seitan, tofu, and all all kinds of vegetables and leafy greens.

Double boiler. Method of indirect cooking that is very handy for cooking foods that burn easily, since the heat is transferred gently and constantly. Generally, the more delicate the ingredient, the gentler the boiling should be. To use this method, you place the food in one receptacle, and then place that in a larger receptacle full of water. For the best results, it's better to use less water to avoid splashing or moving the container with the food more than is necessary.

Gratin. This technique consists in browning certain parts of a food or dish by taking advantage of an oven's overhead grill. Generally, this is used for making pastas, vegetable dishes, and soufflés. This substantially improves the flavor and texture of the ingredients (artichokes, eggplants, squash).

Baking. Using the oven, you can employ different techniques such as broiling, en papillote, and salt-baking. It is important to control the temperature of the oven at all times during the cooking process.

Moist heat cooking

Steaming. This technique is perfect for almost completely preserving the nutrients in the cooked food. It consists of cooking different ingredients using the heat from water vapor, without the food coming in contact with the water below. This is one of the healthiest cooking techniques, because it does not require fatty elements, and it preserves the flavor, texture, and aroma of the ingredients. To steam food, you need a pot and a metal or bamboo steamer basket that will sit inside it. You can also use an electric steamer with a thermostat that will allow you to program the cooking time without having to constantly check on the heat. Other possibilities include the popular Thermomix (that has a function for this kind of cooking) or a combi steamer. Foods like broccoli, artichokes, or beans are left exquisitely prepared when using this simple technique.

Blanc, or white sauce. Some vegetables (like artichokes, endives, and chard) oxidize and turn brown when diced. In order to recover their original color, you can cook them in a blanc, or white sauce. This consists of cooking [p.80] the vegetables in a mix of flour, lemon juice, and water, that will prevent the oxidizing process. The recommended amounts are 1 tablespoon of flour and the juice from 1 lemon for every 2 liters (about 2 quarts) of water.

Boiling. One of the techniques used most often on a daily basis, as well as one of the healthiest. You boil starting with cold water (for foods that require a longer cooking time, such as legumes) or with hot water (you put the ingredients once the water has reached a boil). This technique has the disadvantage of causing the loss of a good part of the nutrients in the ingredients, especially of water-soluble vitamins and minerals that, because of the heat, remain in the liquid used for boiling the food. At any rate, though, you can always use the leftover water to make soups and sauces.

Scalding or blanching. This consists of a quick dunk in a good amount of boiling water. The cook time can vary between just a few seconds and up to 2 minutes, depending on the ingredient. This should be followed immediately by quickly cooling down the food in cold water to halt the cooking process. Blanching is especially used for cooking vegetables and leafy greens to keep them from darkening, or losing texture, aroma, or vitamins when cutting or peeling them. In order to blanch, you need a pot of boiling water and a similarly-sized receptacle full of ice cold water (you can put ice cubes directly in the water to cool it down).

Poaching. This consists of cooking food in some liquid at a temperature below boiling point (100°C or 212°F), unlike blanching, which is done in boiling water. As a general rule, poaching is usually done at a temperature of 80°C, or 176°F, also known as the simmering point.

Cooking with fat

Browning. This is done by superficially cooking food by broiling, frying, baking, or using any other dry heat method until the ingredients take on a characteristic "golden" color.

Frying. This is one of the quickest and tastiest cooking methods, but at the cost of being less healthy. This method causes the food to absorb a part of the fat, which makes it gain more calories. The best fat for frying is olive oil, because it stands up to high heat better than other fats, as well as being less absorbent.

Sauté. This quick cooking technique is usually applied to vegetables before adding them to a stew, sauce, or other dish that requires a long cooking time. Sautéing is usually done in a pot or frying pan, at high heat, without exceeding 100°C (or 212°F) with finely chopped ingredients, and just enough oil to lightly coat them. During the process, you should constantly move the pan so that the heat is evenly distributed to avoid burning any food.

Stir-fry. For this technique you will need a wide skillet that will let you cook the ingredients in a single layer, without piling up on each other. It should also have high sides so that the food doesn't fall out due to the movement of the skillet. This requires little oil, and a high amount of heat applied for a short amount of time. To keep the ingredients from burning, it's important to constantly move the skillet. This way, you will also get the ingredients to cook evenly. The movement is done by firmly gripping the handle of the pan and rocking it back and forth repeatedly and energetically. If you prefer, you can use a spatula to move the ingredients around without lifting the pan from the heat.

Sweating. This technique is similar to sautéing, but it uses less heat so that the food is cooked slowly, bit by bit.

Combination cooking

Stewing. This culinary technique is used to cook foods that require a slow and prolonged cooking time to leave them nice and tender. You can stew all types of vegetables, leafy greens, and legumes without having to sauté them first.

Braising. This technique combines cooking in fat (oil) and wet heat cooking (water). First, you sauté the ingredients, then you mix them with a broth or sauce, and finally cook them over low heat for a long time. This is one of the most popular techniques for making exquisite spoon-tender dishes.

Myths be gone!

eganism is surrounded by myths that are a far cry from reality. Here are some of the most repeated rumors:

The vegan diet causes anemia: FALSE. It is true that not consuming enough vitamin B12 (which is found principally in animal-based products) can create deficiencies in the body, but most vegans simply avoid this by eating foods enriched with this vitamin. The Vegan Society recommends doing one of the following:

- Consuming enriched foods 2 or 3 times a day to obtain at least 3 micrograms of daily B12.

- Taking a daily B12 supplement that supplies at least 10 micrograms of the vitamin.

- Taking a weekly B12 supplement that supplies at least 2,000 micrograms.

Vegans who consume an adequate amount of enriched foods or B12 supplements are less likely to suffer from B12 vitamin deficiencies than people who routinely eat meat.

It is counter-productive for children to follow a vegan diet: FALSE. The vegan diet contains enough varied nutrients for the smallest members of the household to grow up strong and healthy. The regular consumption of energy-packed foods (cereals, nuts, legumes) along with fruits and vegetables, will provide a satisfactory amount of protein.

Milk and its derivatives are essential sources of calcium: TRUE. However, vegan foods such as cereals, seaweed, nuts, and legumes all have excellent calcium absorption rates and, additionally, contain no cholesterol or saturated fats.

Eating meat is the best way to obtain iron: FALSE. This nutrient is especially present in cereals, nuts, green leafy vegetables, and tofu. You can dispense with meat without fear of reducing your body's intake of iron.

The vegan diet is boring: FALSE. The best tool for refuting this myth is the book you are currently holding. There is an infinite number of sweet and savory dishes that you can prepare every day without risk of your diet becoming monotonous or boring. Cooking, whether vegan or not, is based on imagination, and the key lies in knowing how to combine ingredients in appetizing and creative ways.

It is hard to become a vegan: FALSE. In this book, we recommend doing it bit by bit, "vegetizing" menus and progressively eliminating all animal-based ingredients. After some time, and without even realizing it, you'll be eating a one hundred percent vegan diet.

Being vegan means being an animal rights activist: FALSE. Most animal rights defenders do abstain from eating meat because of ethical concerns. However, this does not mean that every person who follows this diet does it for this reason. Other motives could be driven by health concerns, respect for the planet, or for simple pleasure.

FIRST COURSES:

Smoked hummus with raw garlic (p. 90) Baba ghanoush (p. 92) Walnut and mushroom pâté (p. 94) Leek and pine nut pâté (p. 96) Raw cheese plate (p. 99) Butternut squash and parsnip cream (p. 100) Broccoli and almond cream (p. 102) Fried corn soup (p. 104) Onion soup with garlic bread (p. 106) Shiitake, lime, and saffron soup (p. 108) Asparagus with onion jam (p. 111) Olivier salad (p. 112) Fried polenta with barbecue sauce (p. 114) Beet ravioli with raw cheese (p. 116) Roasted artichokes with herb oil (p. 118) Carrot, orange, and pine nut cream (p. 120) Soba noodle and sweet potato salad (p. 123) Fennel and pineapple salad (p. 124) Lentil salad with vinaigrette (p. 126) Fried tofu salad with Caesar dressing (p. 128) Corn patties (p .130) Tubers with three sauces (p. 133)

Smoked hummus with raw garlic

6 people ¦ 45 minutes ¦ Difficulty ✳

Ingredients

500 g (about 1 lb) of cooked garbanzos

2 cloves of garlic

½ teaspoon of powdered cumin

2 tablespoons of tahini

The juice from 2 lemons

2 tablespoons of olive oil

6 tablespoons of water

A pinch of salt

A pinch of pepper

3 stalks of celery

Olive oil

1 teaspoon of smoked paprika

1 Mix the garbanzos and minced garlic with the cumin, tahini, lemon juice, oil, and water, along with salt and pepper. Combine using a mixer until you have achieved a creamy paste.

2 Peel and cut the celery in thin strips.

3 Serve the hummus with a drizzle of oil, some of the smoked paprika, and the strips of celery.

Tahini is a delicious paste made from sesame that can be easily prepared at home. To do this, you just need to toast the sesame seeds a little bit in a hot skillet without oil, constantly keeping them moving so that they don't burn. Next, carefully crush the seeds while adding water little by little until you achieve the desired consistency.

Baba ghanoush

6 people ¦ 15 minutes ¦ Difficulty *

Ingredients

2 eggplants
2 cloves of garlic
1 lemon
3 tablespoons of tahini
1 teaspoon of salt
3 tablespoons of sunflower oil
A pinch of paprika
Olive oil

1 Evenly smoke the eggplant by moving them back and forth over a low flame.

2 In a mixer bowl, mix and crush the cloves of garlic, the lemon juice, the tahini, the salt, and the sunflower oil.

3 Open the smoked eggplant and remove the inside, throwing away the skin. Crush the pulp with the help of a fork and add it to the tahini mixture.

4 Serve the baba ghanoush with a little oil and paprika on top.

Baba ganoush or mutabal, is a delicious eggplant pâté very common in Arabic cooking. It can be eaten by itself or with pita bread or toast.

If you prefer...
You can roast the **eggplant** beforehand in an oven preheated to 180°C or 350°F.

Walnut and mushroom pâté

6 people ¦ 15 minutes ¦ Difficulty ✳

Ingredients

1 onion

3 cloves of garlic

1 tablespoon of olive oil

500 g (about 1 lb) of mushrooms

80 g (about 3 oz) of peeled walnuts

1 teaspoon of brewer's yeast

A pinch of salt

A pinch of pepper

1 Peel and cut the onion and garlic into thin slices.

2 Heat the oil in a pan and brown the onion and garlic over low heat for 2 minutes.

3 Thinly slice the mushrooms and add them to the pan. Cook on medium heat until the mushrooms start to brown.

4 Toast the walnuts in a 180°C (350°F) oven for 2 minutes.

5 In a mixer bowl, mix and crush the ingredients from the pan with the brewer's yeast, a pinch of salt, and a pinch of pepper.

6 Add the walnuts and keep mixing until you achieve a fine, homogeneous cream.

7 Serve the pâté along with some slices of bread.

Mushrooms should be washed well with water to remove the leftover bits of dirt and filth. Once clean, they can be eaten raw in delicious salads, or sautéed in olive oil.

Pine nut and leek pâté

6 people ¦ 40 minutes ¦ Difficulty *

Ingredients

2 blocks of hard tofu

3 tablespoons of sunflower oil

1 tablespoon of olive oil

3 leeks

80 g (about 3 oz) of pine nuts—about ⅓ cup

2 tablespoons of brewer's yeast

1 tablespoon of soy sauce

1 clove of garlic

A pinch of salt

A pinch of pepper

1 teaspoon of smoked paprika

Carrots

Toasted almonds

1 Cut the tofu into cubes and place them in a baking dish with the sunflower oil. Bake at 180°C (350°F) for 25 minutes.

2 Heat a pan with oil and sauté the leeks, after cutting them into slices, until they become transparent.

3 Toast the pine nuts in the oven at 180°C, or 350°F, for 1 minute.

4 In a mixer bowl, mash the leeks, the tofu, the brewer's yeast, the soy sauce, and the garlic together. Season with salt and pepper.

5 Add the pine nuts and serve the pâté with a bit of smoked paprika along with some carrot slices. Garnish with toasted almond pieces.

There are three kinds of tofu, which vary by the amount of water they contain:
» **Soft tofu.** This has the greatest amount of water. It's ideal for making sauces.
» **Hard tofu.** It is denser and normally added to all kinds of soups.
» **Extra hard tofu.** The most dense, it can be sliced, diced, and sautéed, fried, or boiled.

Raw "cheese" plate

6 people ¦ 2 hours and 20 minutes ¦ Difficulty ✳

Ingredients

500 g (about 1 lb) of
pine nuts

4 tablespoons of
brewer's yeast

Juice of 3 lemons

1 teaspoon of salt

1 teaspoon of pepper

4 tarragon leaves

3 dried tomatoes

2 basil leaves

1 lime

2 apples

1 cucumber

Grapes

1 Soak the pine nuts for a couple of hours. Strain and reserve the
water in a bowl.

2 Blend the pine nuts with the brewer's yeast, the lemon juice, and
the salt and pepper. Add a drizzle of the reserved water from the
pine nuts until the mixture becomes a fine, uniform paste.

3 Separate the resulting raw "cheese" into 3 equal parts.

4 Chop and mix the tarragon leaves with one of portions of cheese.

5 Chop and mix the dried tomatoes and the basil leaves with
another portion of cheese.

6 Next, grate the lime skin and mix it with the third portion of
cheese.

7 Cut the apples into small pieces.

8 Cut the cucumber into thin slices.

9 Serve the cheeses on a plate, accompanied by the apple, the
cucumber, and the grapes.

Butternut squash and parsnip cream

6 people ┊ 20 minutes ┊ Difficulty *

Ingredients

2 Figueres or red onions

2 cloves of garlic

250 g (about ½ lb) of butternut squash

80 g (about 3 oz) of parsnips

+ 3 extra parsnips

Salt, pepper, and olive oil

1 Peel and cut the onion and garlic into small pieces. Toss them and sweat them over low heat in a pot with oil.

2 Peel and cut the butternut squash and the 80 g (3 oz) of parsnips into small pieces. Stir into the sautéed onion and garlic and continue cooking over low heat for a couple of minutes.

3 Fill the pot with water to cover the squash, add a pinch of salt and pepper, and cook over medium heat until the squash is nice and soft.

4 Peel and cut the remaining 3 parsnips into thin strips. Cover them with a good amount of salt and let them sit for 5 minutes. Wash the salt off with plenty of water and let the parsnips dry, wrapped in paper towels.

5 Heat up a skillet with plenty of oil and fry the parsnips. Take them off the heat and move them to a bowl lined with paper towels to drain off the excess oil.

6 Blend the squash and parsnip mixture until it achieves a creamy texture.

7 Finally, serve the cream with a drizzle of olive oil, a pinch of pepper, and the fried parsnips.

The Figueres onion is recognizable for the distinct pink color of its skin. Its soft consistency, sweet flavor, and crunchy texture make it perfect for eating fresh.

Broccoli and almond cream

6 people ┆ 25 minutes ┆ Difficulty ✳

Ingredients

1 Figueres onion

2 cloves of garlic

2 tablespoons of olive oil

50 ml (about ¼ cup) of white wine

2 heads of broccoli

100 g (3.5 oz) of toasted almonds

1 slice of "country bread"—good quality rustic bread, such as French or peasant

A pinch of salt

A pinch of pepper

1 Peel and cut the onion and garlic into very small pieces.

2 Heat the oil in a saucepan and sauté the garlic and onion for 3 minutes at medium heat.

3 Add the white wine and let it boil for 1 minute.

4 Remove the stalks from the broccoli and add it to the saucepan. Add water to cover the broccoli by about three fingers and let it boil for 5 minutes.

5 Add 90 g (about 3 oz) of the almonds, the peasant bread, salt, and pepper. Using a blender, blend the ingredients until you achieve a smooth, uniform consistency.

6 Serve the cream along with the rest of the almonds and a little bit of olive oil.

Broccoli is one of the most nutritious and low-calorie vegetables. The best time to eat it is during the spring and winter months.

Fried corn soup

6 people ¦ 30 minutes ¦ Difficulty *

Ingredients

1 onion

2 cloves of garlic

1 teaspoon of sunflower oil

2 red tomatoes

1 teaspoon of paprika

2 l (about 2 quarts) of water

A pinch of chipotle pepper (optional)

A pinch of salt

A pinch of pepper

100 g (3.5 oz) of corn or tortilla chips—about ½ cup

2 avocados

1 Peel and cut the onion and garlic into small pieces.

2 Heat the oil in a saucepan and brown the onion and garlic over low heat.

3 Cut the tomatoes into small pieces, add them to the pan, and continue sautéing the mixture over low heat for about 5 more minutes.

4 Add the paprika, mix everything up, and add the water and chipotle pepper.

5 Bring the soup to a boil, add salt and pepper, and turn the heat down. Cover the pot and cook for another 5 minutes.

6 Lightly crush the corn or tortilla chips and add the pieces to the soup.

7 Finally, serve the soup in bowls along with some slices of avocado.

Onion soup with garlic bread

6 people ¦ 30 minutes ¦ Difficulty *

Ingredients

2 sweet or Vidalia onions

2 green onions

2 Figueres onions

2 white onions

3 cloves of garlic

250 ml (1 cup) of sparkling wine

1 bay leaf

2 tablespoons of olive oil

A pinch of salt

A pinch of pepper

A pinch of chives

For the bread:

6 slices of country bread

125 ml (½ cup) of olive oil

2 cloves of garlic

A pinch of salt

1 Peel and cut the onions and garlic into thin slices.

2 Heat the oil in a saucepan and brown the garlic over low heat for a couple of minutes.

3 Add the onions and continue cooking over low heat for another 10 minutes, stirring constantly to avoid the ingredients sticking to the bottom.

4 Add the sparkling wine and the bay leaf. Keep cooking over low heat until the alcohol has completely evaporated.

5 Add water to the pot until it reaches twice as high as the onions and season with salt and pepper. Cover and cook on low for 5 minutes after it reaches a boil.

6 To get the bread ready, blend the ½ cup of olive oil together with the peeled garlic and a pinch of salt until the mixture is liquid.

7 Spread the bread with the garlic oil mixture and then bake for 5 minutes at 180°C, or 350°F.

8 Serve the soup along with a piece of bread and chopped chives on top.

Shiitake, lime, and saffron soup

6 people ¦ 25 minutes ¦ Difficulty ✳

Ingredients

6 threads of saffron

1 carrot

2 stalks of green garlic—scallions or garlic scapes

2 tablespoons of olive oil

1 l (about 1 quart) of water

200 g (7 oz) of shiitakes

1 lime

A pinch of salt

A pinch of pepper

1 tablespoon of sesame oil

1　Heat up a skillet and toast the saffron threads.

2　Peel and slice the carrot and green garlic.

3　Heat the olive oil in a pot and brown the carrot slices over medium heat for 3 minutes. Add the green garlic and cook for an additional 2 minutes.

4　Add the water, the whole shiitakes, and the lime peel. Season with salt and pepper and cook over low heat until it boils. Continue cooking for 10 more minutes.

5　Serve the soup with a drizzle of sesame oil.

If you prefer...

The jam will have a more intense flavor if you add a splash of vinegar when the onion and sugar are caramelizing.

Asparagus with onion jam

6 people ¦ 25 minutes ¦ Difficulty *

Ingredients

5 Figueres onions

3 tablespoons of brown sugar

42 asparagus spears (7 spears per person)

6 slices of country bread

2 cloves of garlic

12 cherry tomatoes

Olive oil

Salt and pepper

1 Peel and cut the onions into thin slices.

2 In a pot, cook the onions and the brown sugar over low heat until all the liquid reduces and the sugar caramelizes. Set aside the resulting jam.

3 Boil the asparagus for 30 seconds and immediately cool it down in cold water.

4 Heat a bit of oil in a grill pan and lightly brown the asparagus. Take it off the heat and season with salt and pepper.

5 Serve the asparagus on top of the bread slices smeared with garlic, with a bit of the jam, two cherry tomatoes, olive oil, salt, and pepper.

The **asparagus** can be steamed, fried, grilled, roasted, baked au gratin—mind you, it should be served hot or warm, since it loses a large part of its delicious flavor when cold. Likewise, if it's served along with some sort of sauce, this should be hot as well.

Olivier salad

6 people ¦ 30 minutes ¦ Difficulty ✱

Ingredients

100 g, or 3.5 oz, of carrots—about 2 medium

200 g, or 7 oz, of potatoes—about 2 medium

100 g, or 3.5 oz, of black, pitted olives—about ½ cup

⅓ cup of sugar-free soy milk

1 cup of sunflower oil

The juice from 1 lemon

A pinch of salt

A pinch of pepper

100 g, or 3.5 oz, of fresh, peeled peas—about ½ cup

1 Peel and cut the carrots and potatoes in rough chunks. Heat water in two pots and boil the vegetables separately until they are nice and tender. Set aside in the refrigerator.

2 Roughly chop the olives.

3 Mix the soy milk with the sunflower oil, add the lemon juice, and season with salt and pepper. Set the mayonnaise aside in the refrigerator.

4 In a bowl, mix the potatoes, carrots, olives, peas, and the mayonnaise. Season with salt and pepper and serve.

Unlike cow's milk, **soy milk** does not contain lactose, casein (lactic protein), vitamin B12, saturated fats, or cholesterol. In addition to this, it also contains less sodium and fewer calories. It is perfect for making all kinds of creams, sauces, shakes, ice creams, etc.

If you prefer...
Instead of peas, you may use
freshly peeled broad beans,
sweet potatoes, or roasted
peppers

Fried polenta with barbecue sauce

6 people ¦ 40 minutes ¦ Difficulty ✳

Ingredients

½ cup of polenta
2 cups of water
A bit of thyme
A pinch of salt
A pinch of pepper

For the sauce:
2 red onions
100 g (3.5 oz) of brown
sugar—about ½ cup
125 ml (½ cup) of sherry
vinegar
30 g (1 oz) of raisins
A pinch of salt
1 tablespoon of
smoked paprika

1 Boil the two cups of water and add the polenta, thyme, salt, and pepper. Mix well and cook over low heat with the pot covered for 20 minutes.

2 Put the polenta in a lightly oiled container and let it cool down.

3 To make the barbecue sauce, peel and chop the onions, then put them on to boil with the sugar, the vinegar, the raisins, and the salt. Keep cooking over medium heat until the vinegar has completely evaporated.

4 Add the smoked paprika and blend with a hand blender until you achieve a smooth, uniform sauce. Let this cool in the refrigerator.

5 Cut the polenta into long strips, like French fries, and fry in plenty of oil.

6 Serve the fried polenta alongside the barbecue sauce.

Polenta is a semolina made from corn from the north of Italy. It is heavy in calories and very rich in B-type vitamins.

Beet ravioli with raw cheese

6 people ⦙ 35 minutes ⦙ Difficulty ✳

Ingredients

300 g (10.5 oz) of macadamia nuts—about 1 ½ cups

3 tablespoons of brewer's yeast

1 teaspoon of salt

A pinch of pepper

1 lemon

3 tarragon leaves

1 Figueres onion

3 raw beets

For the sauce:

2 red peppers

½ cup of pistachios

½ cup of green onion or scallion

1 clove of garlic

A pinch of salt

A pinch of pepper

1 Allow the nuts to soak for 3 hours. Strain and reserve the water in a bowl.

2 Using a hand blender, blend the nuts with the brewer's yeast, the salt, the pepper, the lemon juice, and the tarragon. Add the leftover water from soaking the nuts bit by bit until you achieve a creamy consistency.

3 To make the sauce, open the red peppers, remove the seeds, and blend with the pistachios, green onion, garlic, salt, and pepper.

4 Peel and cut the Figueres onion and beets into very thin slices.

5 Serve each beet slice with a teaspoon of the nut ricotta and some of the pepper, pistachio, and green onion sauce.

Roasted artichokes with herb oil

6 people ¦ 40 minutes ¦ Difficulty ✻

Ingredients

1 bunch of fresh basil (about 2 ounces)

1 bunch of fresh rosemary (2 full sprigs or 1 ounce)

1 bunch of fresh parsley (about 2 ounces)

1 bunch of fresh thyme (about 1 ounce)

2 cloves of garlic

300 ml (1 ¼ cup) of olive oil

2 teaspoons of salt

12 artichokes

3 ripe tomatoes

A pinch of pepper

1 Using an electric blender, blend all the herbs together.

2 Add the olive oil, the garlic, and the salt, and continue blending until there are no lumps. Pour the herb oil into a large bowl.

3 Cut off half of the stem of the artichokes and remove the outer leaves. Cut the artichokes into quarters and dunk them in the herb oil.

4 Let the artichokes marinate for 15 minutes and then place them in a baking dish.

5 Cover the dish with aluminum foil and bake in a 180°C (350°F) oven for 20 minutes.

6 Sprinkle artichokes with a pinch of pepper and serve with sliced tomatoes.

Artichokes are a vegetable that can be cooked many different ways: boiled, steamed, fried, battered, braised, sautéed, grilled, or baked. Be mindful that when cutting and manipulating artichokes, the leaves can easily oxidize. To avoid this, you should rub them with half a lemon or spritz them with a bit of vinegar.

Carrot, orange, and pine nut cream

6 people ¦ 30 minutes ¦ Difficulty *

Ingredients

2 cloves of garlic

1 tablespoon of olive oil

1 teaspoon of grated ginger

1 onion

9 carrots

The zest of ½ an orange

2 teaspoons of salt

1 teaspoon of pepper

water

50 g (about 2 oz) of pine nuts

olive oil

1 carton of oat milk (substitute other grain or nut milk, optional)

1 Peel and cut the garlic into thin slices.

2 Heat 1 tablespoon of olive oil in a saucepan over low heat. Add the garlic and ginger.

3 Peel and cut the onion into small pieces and add to the sauté.

4 Peel and slice the carrots and add them to the mixture that is cooking.

5 Keep cooking the ingredients for another 5 minutes, until the carrots start looking lightly browned.

6 Add the orange zest.

7 Add the salt, pepper, and water until the ingredients are totally covered. Cook over medium heat for 10 minutes.

8 Blend the mixture until it becomes a smooth cream.

9 Serve the cream along with the pine nuts, a drizzle of olive oil, and a tablespoon of the oat milk.

Soba noodle and sweet potato salad

6 people ¦ 25 minutes ¦ Difficulty *

Ingredients

6 packages of soba noodles

2 sweet potatoes

1 head of leaf lettuce, red oak preferred

12 asparagus spears

2 tablespoons of olive oil

1 sheet of nori seaweed

150 g (about 5 oz) of salted peanuts

For the vinaigrette:

125 ml (½ cup) of sunflower oil

70 ml (about ⅓ cup) of rice vinegar

1 sweet onion

1 tablespoon of miso

1 tablespoon of soy sauce

2 tablespoons of tahini

1 In a pot full of water, cook the noodles over medium heat until they are soft, approximately 4 minutes.

2 Peel and dice the sweet potatoes. Heat a pot full of water and add the sweet potato. Cook for about 8 minutes and immediately dunk in cold water.

3 Cut, wash, and set the lettuce aside until it is nice and dry.

4 Cut the asparagus into quarters and sauté in a skillet in hot oil.

5 Cut the nori seaweed into strips.

6 To make the vinaigrette, mix and blend all the ingredients until there are no lumps left.

7 In the bottom of a bowl, place a few of the red oak leaf lettuce leaves.

8 On top of these, place the noodles, peanuts, sweet potato, asparagus, and seaweed strips. Fill several small bowls with enough of the vinaigrette for each dinner guest.

Fennel and pineapple salad

6 people ⦙ 15 minutes ⦙ Difficulty *

Ingredients

3 fennel bulbs

water

Juice of 4 limes

1 tablespoon of salt

1 pineapple

60 g (2 oz) of almonds—peeled marcona, preferred

60 g (2 oz) of roasted peanuts

1 cup corn kernels—fresh, preferred (about 2 ears of corn)

A pinch of salt

A pinch of pepper

2 limes

1 Using a mandolin or a very sharp knife, slice the fennel bulbs.

2 Fill a bowl halfway with water and add the lime juice and 1 tablespoon of salt.

3 Peel and dice the pineapple. Sauté the fruit in a pan over high heat until it is nice and browned.

4 Chop the almonds and peanuts.

5 Cut the remaining two limes into halves (for garnish).

6 On a tray, place the corn salad down as a base, then the fennel, the pineapple, and the nuts.

7 Season with salt and pepper and garnish with the lime.

Lentil salad with vinaigrette

6 people ¦ 10 minutes ¦ Difficulty ✳

Ingredients

1 tablespoon of white wine vinegar

2 tablespoons of olive oil

2 teaspoons of salt

100 g (3.5 oz) of dried apricots

1 celery stalk

1 red pepper

100 g (3.5 oz) of dried tomatoes

2 avocados

2 Golden Delicious apples

300 g (10.5 oz) of cooked lentils—about 1 ½ cups

2 packages of arugula—about 4 ounces

1 In a large bowl, mix together the vinegar, oil, and salt.

2 Roughly chop and add the apricots.

3 Thinly slice and add the celery.

4 Add the red pepper and the dried tomatoes, diced into small pieces.

5 Next, peel and dice the avocados and add them too.

6 Peel and cut the apples into half-moon shaped slices and add them along with the lentils.

7 Place 4 apple slices and a bit of arugula on each dish. Finally, use two spoons to scoop the ingredients out of the bowl and serve them on top of the arugula and apple slices.

Fried tofu salad with Caesar dressing

6 people ¦ 30 minutes ¦ Difficulty *

Ingredients

2 blocks of tofu
1 baguette
2 cloves of garlic
1 tablespoon of olive oil
1 head of romaine lettuce

For the sauce:
250 ml (1 cup) of soy milk
500 ml (2 cups) of sunflower oil
1 teaspoon of salt
1 lemon
½ tablespoon of Dijon mustard
1 clove of garlic
1 teaspoon capers or 4 large caper-berries

1 Cut the tofu into strips and place them in a baking dish with a little bit of oil.

2 Bake at 180°C (350°F) until the tofu starts to look golden brown.

3 Cut the bread into cubes and place in a different baking dish.

4 Bake the bread at 180°C (350°F) until it is lightly toasted.

5 Rub the bread with the garlic cloves so it absorbs their aroma. Drizzle the tablespoon of oil on top and lightly stir the bread so that it soaks it all up.

6 Wash and cut the lettuce into large chunks and place them inside a bowl. Add the croutons and the tofu on top.

7 Using a blender, mix and emulsify the soy milk and sunflower oil until you get a mayonnaise-like consistency. Add the salt, the squeezed lemon, the mustard, the garlic clove, and the capers, and emulsify again until you are left with a smooth, uniform dressing.

8 Serve the salad along with one ladle of the Caesar dressing per person.

Corn patties

6 people ¦ 20 minutes ¦ Difficulty ✱

Ingredients

1 potato
1 zucchini
2 cloves of garlic
Kernels from 2 ears of corn
2 teaspoons of salt
1 tablespoon of olive oil
½ tablespoon of sesame oil
½ cup of bread crumbs
Oil for frying
Mayonnaise
Barbecue sauce

1 Grate the potato and zucchini and place them in a large bowl.

2 Finely chop the garlic and add it to the bowl.

3 Add the corn, salt, olive oil, sesame oil, and bread crumbs.

4 Mix all the ingredients up well, using your hand, until you get a firm dough.

5 Shape the dough into 12 balls and then flatten them until they are the same shape as a hamburger.

6 In a skillet with oil, fry the mini-burgers in batches of three, being careful not to break them.

7 Once they are nice and brown, pat off the excess oil with a paper towel and serve with mayonnaise and barbecue sauce.

Tubers with three sauces

6 people ¦ 45 minutes ¦ Difficulty *

Ingredients

2 parsnips

2 potatoes—Yukon Gold or yellow, preferred

2 beets

1 sweet potato

1 head of garlic

3 tablespoons of olive oil

2 teaspoons of salt

One pinch of black pepper

Caesar dressing

For the aioli:

125 ml (½ cup) of soy milk

250 ml (½ cup) of sunflower oil

1 teaspoon of salt

2 cloves of garlic

1 lemon

For the wild sauce:

180 ml (¾ cup) of aioli

1 tablespoon of smoked paprika

1 Peel and cube all of the tubers and place them in a baking dish.

2 Cut the head of garlic in half and add it to the baking dish.

3 Add the oil, salt, and pepper. Mix well.

4 Cover the dish with aluminum foil and bake in a 180°C (350°F) oven for 25 minutes.

5 Using an electric blender, emulsify the soy milk, the sunflower oil, and the salt until a mayonnaise forms.

6 Add the garlic cloves and the lemon. Continue emulsifying until you have a smooth, uniform aioli.

7 Add the smoked paprika to the aioli and mix.

8 Serve the tubers on a tray alongside the Caesar dressing, the aioli, and the wild sauce.

Yukon Gold potatoes are perfect for frying or baking. They are known for their smooth, yellow skin. This is one of the most sought after varieties for cooking.

Parsnips are a similar vegetable to carrots, although their texture is not as crunchy and watery. They are often used for making soups, broths, and purees.

SECOND COURSES:

Seitan with cream, roasted sweet potato,
and caramelized onion

6 people ¦ 30 minutes ¦ Difficulty **

Ingredients

Olive oil

12 seitan fillets

2 packages vegetable cream cheese spread

Salt and pepper

3 sweet potatoes

3 red onions

Sugar

1 Heat a bit of oil in a grill pan and lightly brown the seitan.

2 Add the cream along with a pinch of salt and pepper. Continue cooking over medium heat for a couple more minutes.

3 Wrap the sweet potatoes separately in aluminum foil and place them in an oven preheated to 180°C (350°F) for 20 minutes or until they are soft.

4 Cut the onions into slices and cook them in a covered pot over low heat with a bit of sugar until they start to caramelize.

5 Cut the sweet potato into slices and serve them alongside the caramelized onion and the seitan with cream.

Seitan has an elevated protein content, but is also low in calories, helps reduce cholesterol, and has much more calcium and vitamins than meat.

If you prefer...

Instead of sweet potatoes, you may use small chunks of butternut squash that you will also roast in the oven.

Seitan piccata with creamy spinach

6 people ¦ 40 minutes ¦ Difficulty **

Ingredients

For the spinach:
½ block of smoked tofu
½ of natural tofu
2 tablespoons
of brewer's yeast
2 cloves of garlic
1 onion
250 g (½ lb) of mushrooms
1 bag of frozen spinach
400 ml (about 1 and
¾ cups) of vegetable broth
Oil

For the sauce:
Oil
6 garlic cloves
1 cup of white wine
½ l (about 2 cups) of
vegetable broth
2 lemons
½ teaspoon capers
(or 3 large caper-berries)
2 tablespoons of
brewer's yeast
1 teaspoon of corn meal
(corn flour preferred)
Salt

For the fillets:
12 seitan fillets
2 cups of whole wheat flour
1 cup of bread crumbs
1 tablespoon of thyme
1 tablespoon of oregano
1 tablespoon of salt
1 tablespoon of pepper
1 tablespoon of mustard

1 For the spinach, blend up both types of tofu with the brewer's yeast in a bowl. Little by little, add water until the texture is smooth and creamy.

2 In a pan with a tablespoon of oil, sweat the garlic and the chopped onion. When they start to brown, add the mushrooms, sliced.

3 Add the spinach and 250 ml (1 cup) of the vegetable broth and let it reduce slowly until there is barely any water left. Add the tofu cream and cook over very low heat with the pot covered well for 3 minutes. Add salt and pepper and set aside.

4 Now it's time to make the sauce. In a pan with 1 tablespoon of oil, sweat the peeled and chopped garlic. Add the wine and reduce it by about half. Add 150 ml (about ⅔ cups) of vegetable broth, the juice of the lemons, the capers, the brewer's yeast, the corn flour (dissolved in a bit of water), and the salt. Let this cook.

5 In a bowl, mix the whole-wheat flour, the bread crumbs, the herbs, and a pinch of salt. In another bowl, mix the mustard with 4 cups of water and whisk it up until there are no lumps left.

6 Using two forks, dredge the seitan in the flour mix first, and then in the mustard. Repeat this step a couple of times, and fry the seitan in batches in a pan with oil. Place the seitan on top of an absorbent paper towel to drain.

7 Put each dish together with the creamy spinach, 2 seitan fillets, and the piccata sauce on top. Garnish with slices of lemon.

Sliced seitan with mushroom sauce,
and potato mille-feuille

6 people ┊ 50 minutes ┊ Difficulty ✳✳

Ingredients

For mille-feuille:
500 g (1 lb) of potatoes
2 onions
4 cloves of garlic, bay
leaves, thyme, salt,
pepper, and oil

For the sauce:
½ bulb of garlic
2 chopped onions
olive oil
2 cups of red wine
250 g (½ lb) of common
mushrooms
250 g (½ lb) of shiitake
mushrooms
1 slice of toasted bread
1 cup of vegetable broth
2 tablespoons of brewer's
yeast, sage, basil, salt,
and pepper

For the fillets:
12 seitan fillets
2 cups of flour
1 cup of bread crumbs
1 tablespoon of thyme
1 tablespoon of oregano
1 tablespoon of salt
1 tablespoon of pepper
2 tablespoons of paprika
4 cups water
½ cup soy sauce

1 Start by making the mille-feuille. To do this, cut the potatoes and onions into slices. Next, cut the garlic cloves into small pieces. In a large bowl, mix them with the herbs (to taste), olive oil, and a pinch of salt and pepper.

2 Put the mixture into a baking dish with aluminum foil and bake at 180°C (350°F) until the potatoes are nice and soft.

3 Continue now with the sauce. Brown the garlic and the chopped onion with a little olive oil. Add the wine and reduce to about ⅓ of its volume.

4 Add the common mushrooms, the shiitakes, and the toasted bread and cook over low heat in a covered pot for about 20 minutes.

5 Add the vegetable broth and cook for 15 minutes. Add the herbs to taste, blend well, and season with salt and pepper.

6 In a bowl, mix the flour, the bread crumbs, the herbs, the paprika, and a pinch of salt. In another bowl, mix the 4 cups of water with a little soy sauce to give it color.

7 Using a pair of forks, dredge the seitan in the flour first, and then in the soy. Repeat this step two times. Fry the seitan in batches in a pan with plenty of oil and let it dry on some paper towels.

8 On a serving plate, lay down some of the sauce first, a piece of the mille-feuille, and the seitan fillets.

Shiitake mushrooms have a lot of fiber, barely any calories, and contain most of the essential amino acids. They're perfect for making broth or for adding to stews.

Seitan shish kebob

6 people ┆ 20 minutes ┆ Difficulty ✳

Ingredients

60 chunks of seitan (evenly cut)

Olive oil

Salt and pepper

Skewers (metal or wooden)

For the marinade:

1 bunch of parsley

1 onion

3 cloves of garlic

3 tablespoons of paprika

Salt

1 cup of olive oil

1 Finely chop the parsley, onion, and garlic, and mix them in a bowl with the paprika, salt, and olive oil.

2 Thread the seitan onto the skewers (2 skewers per dinner guest), and let them sit in the marinade overnight.

3 The next day, heat a pan up with oil and fry the skewers over medium heat. Serve extra hot and accompanied with bread.

✓ *A good trick*
It's best to let the marinade sit overnight so the skewers become more flavorful.

Gnocchi with pepper, walnut,
and basil sauce

6 people ¦ 45 minutes ¦ Difficulty *

Ingredients

2 packages of gnocchi, fresh preferred

2 zucchinis

For the sauce:

3 red peppers

3 cloves of garlic

200 g (7 oz) of walnuts—about ½ cup

1 bunch of basil

½ cup of olive oil

Salt and pepper

1 Start by making the sauce. Put the peppers and the garlic in a baking dish, cover with aluminum foil, and bake at 180°C (350°F) until the peppers are nice and charred.

2 On a separate pan, spread the walnuts and place in oven until they are well toasted.

3 Peel the peppers and the garlic and add them to a blender with the walnuts, basil, oil, salt, and the pepper. Blend until the sauce is uniform.

4 Cut the zucchini into small, uniform cubes. Next, sauté them with a little oil, salt, and pepper.

5 Boil the gnocchi and serve it with 1 tablespoon of the pepper sauce and a bit of zucchini.

Penne with garlic oil, olives,
spinach, and asparagus

6 people ¦ 15 minutes ¦ Difficulty ✳

Ingredients

½ cup of sliced almonds

1 cup of olives

3 bunches of asparagus

8 cloves of garlic

½ cup of olive oil

1 bunch of spinach

600 g (21 oz) of penne pasta

1 Preheat the oven and bake the almonds until they are well toasted.

2 Pit and slice up the olives.

3 Cut the asparagus into crosswise strips, blanch them for 1 minute, and quickly shock them in cold water.

4 Finely dice the garlic cloves.

5 Heat the olive oil in a pan and sauté the asparagus and garlic until they are nicely browned. Turn off the heat and add the spinach, olives, and almonds.

6 Boil the pasta and serve it with the mixture you just made.

✓ *A good trick*
To intensify and add heat to the flavor, you can add a bit of chili pepper.

Tagliatelle with leeks, dried tomatoes, and basil sauce.

6 people ¦ 25 minutes ¦ Difficulty ✳

Ingredients

Olive oil

Salt and pepper

½ cup of white wine

5 leeks, sliced

2 dried tomatoes

5 basil leaves

200 g (7 oz) of pine nuts

660 g (about 23 oz) of tagliatelle pasta

1 In a pot with a little bit of oil, a pinch of salt, pepper, and the wine, braise the sliced leeks until they are nice and tender.

2 Next, blend the mixture in a blender along with the dried tomatoes and basil. Add a bit of water until it achieves a creamy texture.

3 Bake the pine nuts until they are well toasted and add them whole to the leek sauce.

4 Boil the pasta, drain it, and serve it with the sauce.

✓ *A good trick*
To intensify the dish's flavor, add some spices before serving it.

Linguine with butternut squash and capers

6 people ¦ 30 minutes ¦ Difficulty *

Ingredients

1 large butternut squash
Olive oil
1 onion
3 cloves of garlic
1 bottle of beer, dark preferred
Salt and pepper
½ teaspoon capers
(or 3 large caper-berries)
900 g (2 lbs) of linguine

1 Peel and dice the butternut squash.

2 In a pot with hot oil, sweat the onions and the thinly sliced garlic until they are translucent. Add the diced butternut squash, the dark beer, the salt, and the pepper. Keep the pot covered over low heat until the butternut squash is tender.

3 Wash the capers to remove the excess salt and add them to the pot. Keep the pot covered over the heat for another minute and blend the mixture until you have a smooth, uniform sauce. Season with salt and pepper.

4 Boil the linguine and serve it with the butternut squash and caper sauce.

Linguine is a type of pasta very similar to spaghetti and originating from Campania, a region of Italy. Thanks to its shape, this pasta adapts itself well to all kinds of sauces and sides.

Shiitake and artichoke risotto

6 people ¦ 20 minutes ¦ Difficulty *

Ingredients

2 onions
2 cloves of garlic
Olive oil
1 bottle of beer, dark preferred
300 g (10.5 oz) of brown rice—about 1 ½ cups
2 artichokes
250 g (½ lb) of shiitakes
Salt and pepper
Vegetable broth

1 Peel and cut the onion and garlic into very small chunks, and sauté them in a bit of olive oil. Add the beer and continue cooking until it has fully reduced. Mix with the rice.

2 Cut up the artichokes and the garlic. In a pan with oil, sauté and brown the vegetables.

3 Cut the mushrooms into slices and sauté them with a bit of oil and salt until they are nicely browned. Take off the heat and in a separate bowl, mix the mushrooms with the artichokes. Set aside.

4 In a pot with some of the broth, boil the rice until the liquid has reduced approximately by half. Immediately, add a good handful of the mushroom and artichoke mixture.

5 Season with salt and pepper and serve.

Rice sautéed with napa cabbage, yakitori tofu,
and mint-roasted carrots

6 people ┊ 40 minutes ┊ Difficulty ✳

Ingredients

½ a napa cabbage

1 teaspoon of salt

Pepper

Olive oil

300 g (10.5 oz) of brown rice—about 1 ½ cup

1 cup of red wine

¼ cup of soy sauce

½ cup of sugar

1 block of tofu

5 carrots

1 bunch of mint leaves

¼ cup of sunflower oil

2 tablespoons of sesame oil

Fresh spinach, chopped

1 Slice and sauté the napa cabbage with a bit of salt, pepper, and olive oil until it is tender. Mix with the rice.

2 In a bowl, make the yakitori by mixing the wine, the soy sauce, and the sugar until sugar is well dissolved.

3 Cut the tofu into slices and place them in a baking tray with a bit of oil and the yakitori on top. Bake at 180°C (350°F) for 15 minutes or until the tofu is nicely browned.

4 Peel and cut the carrots lengthwise.

5 Blend the mint with the sunflower oil, the sesame oil, and the salt until there are no more lumps.

6 Add the carrots and the mint oil to a baking tray and cook at 180°C (350°F) until the carrots are nice and tender.

7 Serve the rice alongside the tofu, the carrots, and the chopped spinach.

If you prefer...
Instead of mint, you can
add flavor to this dish using
shiso or **meadowsweet**
leaves.

Rice with thyme-roasted butternut squash,
leek sauce, and sautéed walnuts

6 people ¦ 30 minutes ¦ Difficulty *

Ingredients

1 large butternut squash

Thyme

2 cloves of garlic

300 g (10.5 oz) of
walnuts—about 1 ½ cups

3 tablespoons of olive
oil

3 tablespoons of soy
sauce

300 g (10.5 oz) of boiled
brown rice—about
1 ½ cups

For the sauce:

4 leeks

Salt and pepper

½ bottle of white wine

Olive oil

Soy milk

Nutmeg

1 Heat up a pot with olive oil and add the sliced leeks, a pinch of salt, another of pepper, and the wine. Keep over the heat until all the alcohol has been reduced.

2 Blend the mixture in a blender or thermomix and add a bit of soy milk and grated nutmeg to give it a creamier texture.

3 Peel and dice the butternut squash. Place the chunks in a baking tray with the thyme, and the garlic cloves, cover with aluminum foil, and bake at 180°C (350°F) until the butternut squash is nice and tender.

4 Sauté the walnuts with the oil and soy sauce until they start to brown.

5 In a bowl, to be used as a mold, add some of the walnuts, then a layer of butternut squash, and the brown rice on top. Press down well and turn it over onto a plate, being careful to preserve the shape. Add the sauce and serve.

Tofu with sweet and sour sauce,
and vegetables in sesame oil

6 people ┆ 20 minutes ┆ Difficulty ✻

Ingredients

12 tofu fillets
Flour
1 bunch of asparagus
1 head of broccoli
Sesame oil
2 red peppers
1 red onion
2 peeled carrots
Salt and pepper

For the sauce:
¼ pineapple, diced
1 cup of vegetable broth
½ cup of sugar
¼ cup of apple cider vinegar
¼ cup of ketchup
1 teaspoon of corn starch
Salt and pepper

1 Start by making the sweet and sour sauce. To do this, add all the ingredients (except the cornstarch) to a pot and cook over low heat until the vinegar has evaporated completely. Dissolve the cornstarch in a bit of water, then add to the pot, and mix well to keep the sauce from sticking to the bottom.

2 Dredge the tofu fillets in a dish with flour. Next, heat up a pan with plenty of oil and brown the tofu on both sides.

3 Blanch the asparagus and the broccoli for 1 minute in boiling water and quickly shock them in cold water.

4 In a pan, heat up the sesame oil and sauté the peppers, onion, broccoli, asparagus, and carrots. Season with salt and pepper.

5 Finally, serve the sautéed vegetables next to the tofu fillets and sweet and sour sauce.

» **Tofu** is an unmatched source of very high quality vegetable protein and can be fried, battered, stewed, grilled, put in soups, sauces, and even desserts.
» **Sesame oil** is very tasty and aromatic. It is important that it be unrefined, since it will retain all of its nutritional properties (rich in iron, magnesium, and vitamin E).

Red pepper, macadamia nut,
and rosemary pâté

6 people ¦ 35 minutes ¦ Difficulty ✳

Ingredients

5 red peppers

200 g (7 oz) of macadamia nuts— about 1 cup

4 rosemary sprigs

8 tablespoons of olive oil

A pinch of salt

A pinch of pepper

1 Start by charring the peppers whole in the oven at about 180°C (350°F) for 20 minutes. Next, let them cool to room temperature.

2 Roast the walnuts in a 180°C (350°F) oven for 3 minutes.

3 Peel and blend the peppers with the walnuts, the rosemary, the oil, and a pinch of salt and pepper. Blend until the mixture has become a smooth and uniform cream.

4 Serve the pâté accompanied with some raw vegetables or rye bread.

Macadamia, or Queensland, nuts are quite valued for their delicate flavor and smooth texture. They have a high amount of calories (about 700 calories for every 100 g, or 3.5 oz) and are very rich in protein, carbohydrates, and fiber.

Mushroom and rosemary paella

6 people ¦ 45 minutes ¦ Difficulty *

Ingredients

1 onion

2 cloves of garlic

3 tablespoons of olive oil

2 red tomatoes

100 g (3.5 oz) of common mushrooms

100 g (3.5 oz) of oyster mushrooms

6 cups of rice

4 threads of saffron

50 g (a little less than 2 oz) of peas

A pinch of salt

A pinch of pepper

1 sprig of rosemary

Vegetable broth

Parsley or green onion

1 Peel and cut the onion and garlic into very small pieces.

2 Heat the oil in a paella pan and add the garlic and the onion. Cook over medium heat for 2 minutes.

3 Cut the tomatoes into cubes and add them to the paella.

4 Slice both types of mushrooms. Add the mushrooms to the paella and cook for 3 minutes.

5 Add the rice, the saffron, the peas, the salt, the pepper, and the rosemary.

6 Cover the rice with vegetable broth and cook over low heat without moving the ingredients until it's ready.

7 Add some parsley leaves or green onion and serve.

Bean and rice burrito
with guacamole and pico de gallo

6 people ┊ 30 minutes ┊ Difficulty **

Ingredients

1 ½ cups of black beans
4 cloves of garlic
1 bay leaf
2 onions
150 g (½ lb) of crushed tomatoes
1 teaspoon of chipotle powder,
Salt and pepper
Olive oil
6 wheat tortillas
150 g (about 5 oz) of boiled
brown rice
Leafy greens
Jalapeños
Tomato slices

For the guacamole:
4 avocados
2 tomatoes
1 onion
Cilantro leaves
4 lemons
Salt

For the pico de gallo:
2 red peppers
2 tomatoes
1 red onion
A few cilantro leaves
Juice of 1 lemon
Salt

1 Cook the beans with two cloves of garlic, the bay leaf, and a pinch of salt until they are nice and tender. Drain the of excess water.

2 Chop and sweat the onion and the two remaining cloves of garlic in a large pot with olive oil. Add the crushed tomatoes and the chipotle and cook over low heat until part of the broth has evaporated. Add the beans and continue braising over low heat, with the pot covered, for about 20 minutes. Stir occasionally to keep the stew from sticking to the pot. Season with salt and pepper.

3 Move on to the guacamole. Cut up the avocados and put them in a bowl. Chop the tomatoes, the onion, and the cilantro. Mix them with the avocado.

4 Using a fork, mash the whole mixture together and add the lemon juice and a pinch of salt. Continue mashing until you achieve the texture of guacamole.

5 To make the pico de gallo, mix and mash all the ingredients.

6 Fill the wheat tortillas with a bit of rice and a good amount of beans. Roll the burritos up and heat them lightly in the oven before serving, along with the guacamole, pico de gallo, some fresh greens, jalapeños, and some tomato slices.

Vegan hamburger

6 people ┊ 20 minutes ┊ Difficulty *

Ingredients

150 g (about 5 oz) of white beans

150 g (about 5 oz) of red beans

1 red onion

1 clove of garlic

¼ cup of chopped cilantro

¼ cup of chopped parsley

4 basil leaves

1 tablespoon of smoked paprika

1 tablespoon of oregano

1 tablespoon of olive oil

Salt and pepper

2 tablespoons of bread crumbs

1 In a bowl, combine the beans and use a fork to mash them up.

2 Peel and chop the garlic and onion and add them to the beans.

3 Chop and mix the cilantro, parsley, and basil, and add to bean mixture.

4 Add the paprika, the oregano, the oil, and a pinch of salt and pepper. Mix well.

5 Add the bread crumbs bit by bit, kneading the mixture with your hands.

6 Shape and fry 6 hamburgers over medium heat.

Herbs and spices like cilantro, basil, oregano, and paprika are excellent allies of the vegan cook. When used in moderation, they enrich the flavor, texture, and aroma of dishes and allow for multiple combinations.

If you prefer...

Vegan hamburgers can be
served with a little bit of
chipotle and Serrano chilies. Both
varieties are very spicy,
so you might want
to use small amounts.

Raw lasagna

6 people ¦ 40 minutes ¦ Difficulty *

Ingredients

4 zucchinis
2 tomatoes
arugula
salt
pepper
oil

For the ricotta:
2 cups of raw cashews
120 ml (½ cup) of water
3 tablespoons of lemon juice
2 of brewer's yeast
1 of salt

For the sauce:
2 cups of dried tomatoes (soaked for 5 hours)
3 fresh tomatoes
1 onion
30 g (1 oz) of raisins
3 tablespoons of lemon juice
2 tablespoons of oregano
2 tablespoons of thyme
2 tablespoons of salt
2 basil leaves, and a pinch of pepper

For the pesto:
1 bunch of basil
1 cup of raw pistachios
60 ml (¼ cup) of oil
Salt and pepper

1 For the ricotta, grind up the cashews (after soaking them for a couple of hours) and blend with the rest of the ingredients until the texture becomes creamy.

2 Next, make the tomato sauce. Mix and blend all the ingredients.

3 Now on to the pesto. Grind up the pistachios and mix with the rest of the ingredients.

4 To make the lasagna filling, start by finely slicing up the zucchini and the tomatoes.

5 In the bottom of a dish, place two slices of zucchini, add some of the cashew ricotta, 1 slice of tomato, the tomato sauce, and the pistachio pesto. Repeat the pattern on top of the previous one and finish off with 2 slices of zucchini, a bit of arugula, olive oil, salt, and pepper.

» Even though it is considered a nut, cashews are actually the seeds of a tree native to Brazil. They are high in calories and rich in B-type vitamins.

» **Arugula** belongs to the Brussels sprouts family and originates from the Mediterranean basin and from western Asia. Used often in Italian cooking, it is rich in vitamin C, and minerals such as magnesium, potassium, and iron.

Potatoes au gratin

6 people ¦ 50 minutes ¦ Difficulty ✳

Ingredients

1 head of cauliflower
1 head of broccoli
500 g (1 lb) of potatoes
3 onions
2 cloves of garlic
250 ml (1 cup) of
vegetable cream cheese
A pinch of salt
A pinch of pepper
Olive oil
1 tablespoon of bread
crumbs

1 Cut the cauliflower and broccoli into small chunks. Bring a pot of water to boil and cook the chopped vegetables for 3 minutes.

2 Peel and cut the potatoes into very thin slices.

3 Peel and cut the onions and garlic into thin slices.

4 Place the broccoli and the cauliflower into the bottom of a dish and add the cream on top.

5 In a bowl, mix the onions, the garlic, and potatoes. Season with salt and pepper and add the mixture on top of the broccoli and cauliflower.

6 Add more cream, a drizzle of olive oil, and bread crumbs.

7 Cover the dish with aluminum foil and bake for 30 minutes at 180°C (350°F).

✓ *A good trick*
To make this recipe even tastier, you can bake the potatoes in a ceramic dish.

Fried tofu with peanut sauce

6 people ¦ 20 minutes ¦ Difficulty ✻

Ingredients

2 blocks of soft tofu

Olive oil

2 onions

1 tablespoon of sunflower oil

200 g (7 oz) of peanut butter—about 1 cup

200 ml (about 7 fl oz) of water

3 tablespoons of soy sauce

Some cilantro leaves

1 Cut the blocks of tofu into large cubes.

2 Heat the sunflower oil in a pan and fry the tofu cubes in small batches.

3 Peel and cut the onions into thin slices.

4 Heat the olive oil in a pan and add the onions. Fry the onion for 10 minutes over medium heat.

5 In a blender cup, blend the peanut butter, the onions, the water, and the soy sauce until you have a smooth sauce.

6 Thread the fried tofu cubes onto several skewers.

7 Serve with the peanut sauce and some cilantro leaves.

Peanut butter is very rich in nutrients like B and E type vitamins, as well as potassium and magnesium. Mind you, it does contain a considerable amount of protein, so you should eat it with a bit of caution.

Thai tofu

6 people ¦ 40 minutes ¦ Difficulty *

Ingredients

1 block of tofu, diced

Olive oil

2 red onions

2 cloves of garlic

4 carrots

3 tablespoons of sunflower oil

1 teaspoon of grated ginger

1 l (about 34 oz) of coconut milk

1 tablespoon of yellow curry paste

Salt and pepper

½ cup fresh peas—whole sugar snap or snow peas, or shelled English (Field) peas

Some cilantro leaves

1 Fry the diced tofu in olive oil until it is nice and golden.

2 Peel and cut the onions, garlic, and carrots into thin slices.

3 Heat a saucepan with sunflower oil, add the garlic and ginger, and cook over medium heat for 1 minute.

4 Add the onions and cook for 3 minutes.

5 Add the carrots, coconut milk, curry paste, salt, and pepper. Heat over low heat with the pot covered until it comes to a boil. Cook for another 5 minutes.

6 Add the tofu and field peas and cook uncovered for 3 more minutes.

7 Serve the stew with some cilantro leaves.

Field peas, or dun peas, are a type of pod belonging to the same family as peas, and are used often in French gastronomy. They have a pleasant, sweet flavor, and can be boiled, sautéed, or steamed. They stand out thanks to their content of vegetable protein, vitamins B and C, minerals, and fiber.

Drunken meatballs

6 people ¦ 30 minutes ¦ Difficulty ✹✹

Ingredients

3 cloves of garlic
1 bunch of cilantro
1 package of smoked tofu
1 tablespoon of smoked paprika
1 cup of bread crumbs
¼ cup of vegetable broth
1 tablespoon of salt
1 tablespoon of pepper
1 teaspoon of grated ginger
Olive oil

For the braising liquid:
2 cloves of garlic
2 onions
2 carrots
250 ml (1 cup) red wine
2 tablespoons olive oil
3 tablespoons crushed tomatoes
200 ml (8.5 fl oz) vegetable broth
Pepper
Cilantro leaves

1 Start making the meatballs. Peel and dice the garlic.

2 Separate and chop the cilantro leaves using a well sharpened knife.

3 In a bowl, mix the garlic, cilantro, tofu, paprika, bread crumbs, broth, salt, pepper, and ginger until you have a firm dough.

4 With your hands slightly wet, shape several balls out of the resulting dough.

5 Heat oil in a pan and fry the meatballs until they are golden brown.

6 Move on to the braising liquid. Peel and cut the garlic into thin slices.

7 Heat the oil in a pan and fry the garlic.

8 Add the peeled and diced onions. Stir well so that the garlic does not burn.

9 Peel and slice the carrots.

10 To the pan, add the red wine, crushed tomatoes, the sliced carrots, salt, and pepper. Stew over medium heat until the wine has reduced by half.

11 Add the vegetable broth and stir well.

12 Place the meatballs in a dish and pour the wine braising liquid on top. Garnish with a few cilantro leaves.

Pasta with seitan and green pepper

6 people ¦ 25 minutes ¦ Difficulty *

Ingredients

2 packages of seitan

2 green peppers

3 tablespoons of olive oil

500 ml (2 cups) of soy vegetable cream cheese

1 tablespoon of salt

1 teaspoon of pepper

600 g (21 oz) of spaghetti

1 Cut the seitan and peppers into large cubes and set them aside.

2 Heat the oil in a pan over medium heat and fry the peppers for a couple of minutes.

3 Add the seitan and stir well for 5 minutes, being careful not to let anything stick.

4 Add the cream, salt, and pepper. Continue cooking over low heat for 2 minutes.

5 In a large pot, boil the spaghetti until it is al dente.

6 Serve a portion of the pasta with the seitan sauce on top.

7 Season with salt and pepper.

Thanks to its high protein content, **seitan** is highly recommended for athletes or those who are considerably physically active. It is also an excellent food for pregnant women, for infants and adolescents, as well as convalescents.

Polenta with mushrooms

6 people ¦ 50 minutes ¦ Difficulty **

Ingredients

1 l (about 1 quart) of water
1 bulb of garlic
1 carrot
1 onion
1 celery stalk
Chopped rosemary
A pinch of salt
A pinch of pepper
200 g (7 oz) of instant polenta
18 fresh mushrooms—about 1 pound, oyster preferred
Olive oil
250 ml (1 cup) of aioli
1 tablespoon almonds, peeled marcona preferred
Italian sauce, such as Romesco

1 In a pot of boiling water, boil the garlic, the carrot, the onion, and the celery for 10 minutes.

2 Drain the broth and add half of the chopped rosemary, along with a pinch of salt and pepper.

3 Boil the broth with instant polenta (following the package instructions).

4 Spread the polenta in a flat baking dish.

5 Let it rest for 30 minutes and cut out several circles using a cookie cutter.

6 In a baking dish, place 18 of the polenta circles and put 1 oyster mushroom on each one.

7 Using a basting brush, glaze each slice with a bit of oil and add a pinch of salt, pepper, and chopped rosemary.

8 Bake for 10 minutes at 200°C (400°F).

9 Using a blender, mix and emulsify the aioli and almonds.

10 Serve 3 slices of polenta per person, along with some Romesco sauce and almond aioli.

Feijoada

6 people ┆ 35 minutes ┆ Difficulty ✳

Ingredients

2 cloves of garlic

3 tablespoons of vegetable oil

1 carrot

1 zucchini

1 eggplant

1 package of seitan

500 g (about 1 lb) of cooked black beans

250 ml (1 cup) of vegetable broth

1 package of smoked tofu

1 tablespoon of salt

1 teaspoon of pepper

10 parsley leaves

1 Peel and cut the garlic into thin slices.

2 In a pan with oil, lightly fry the garlic.

3 Peel and dice the carrots. Add them to the pan and cook for 3 minutes.

4 Add the zucchini, the eggplant, and the seitan, cut into large cubes. Continue cooking over low heat for 10 minutes with the pan covered.

5 Add the beans and the vegetable broth. Cook for 5 minutes over medium heat.

6 Cut the tofu into large cubes and add to the pan. Turn the heat off, season with salt and pepper, and mix well.

7 Serve the feijoada along with some parsley leaves.

Feijoada is one of the most representative dishes of Brazilian and Portuguese cooking. This dish is very high in calories, so it is best to only eat one serving, preferably during the colder months.

Quinoa stuffed peppers

6 people ¦ 40 minutes ¦ Difficulty **

Ingredients

6 red peppers
½ a head of cauliflower
½ a head of broccoli
3 stalks of green garlic
1.1 l (just over 1 quart) of water
3 cups of quinoa
Parsley
100 g (3.5 oz) of toasted almonds
1 package of tofu

For the sauce:
2 cloves of garlic
A pinch of cumin
2 tablespoons of oil
3 carrots
250 ml (1 cup) of vegetable broth
A pinch of salt
A pinch of pepper

1 Bake the peppers for 20 minutes at 180°C (350°F). Once cooled, remove the skin and the stems.

2 Cut the cauliflower and broccoli into small chunks.

3 Boil the broccoli for 2 minutes. Take out of the water, drain well, and submerge the pieces in cold water.

4 Add the cauliflower to the same water and cook for 4 minutes. Drain well and put the pieces in cold water.

5 In a pan with a bit of oil, salt, and pepper, sauté the sliced green garlic along with the broccoli and cauliflower.

6 In a saucepan, boil the water (1.1 l, or just over 1 quart) with a pinch of salt. When the water starts to boil, add the quinoa and cook over low heat, with the pot covered, for 12 minutes.

7 Chop the parsley and almonds. Mix with the quinoa.

8 Cut the tofu into strips and add to the quinoa.

9 Serve the quinoa in the bottom of a dish with the help of a baking ring and decorate it with the sautéed broccoli and cauliflower.

10 To make the sauce, fry the sliced garlic and the cumin in a pan with oil. Peel and slice the carrots into thin half-moon shapes and add them to the pan. Add the vegetable broth, the salt, and the pepper. Cook for 10 minutes over medium heat. Blend the mixture using an electric blender.

11 Fill each pepper with the quinoa mixture and the vegetables. Serve with the carrot sauce.

Mushroom and pea pie

6 people ⦙ 25 minutes ⦙ Difficulty **

Ingredients

For the dough:

400 g (14 oz) of wheat flour

200 g (7 oz) of margarine

3 tablespoons of ice water

For the filling:

3 tablespoons of olive oil

2 cloves of garlic

2 onions

200 g (7 oz) of mushrooms

2 tablespoons of brandy

100 g (3.5 oz) of peas—about ½ cup

1 teaspoon of salt

1 teaspoon of pepper

6 parsley leaves

80 g (about 3 oz) of cornstarch—about ¼ cup

80 g (about 3 fl oz) of water—about ⅓ cup

1 Mix all the dough ingredients in a bowl until they form a uniform dough. Wrap with plastic film and set aside in the fridge while you make the stew.

2 In a pan with oil, fry the peeled and sliced garlic for 2 minutes.

3 Add the peeled and diced onions to the pan. Cook for 4 minutes.

4 Add the sliced mushrooms and the brandy. Cook over medium heat for 5 minutes, stirring carefully to keep the mixture from sticking.

5 Finally, add the peas, the salt, the pepper, and the parsley leaves. Turn the heat off and stir well.

6 Mix the cornstarch with the water and add to the stew.

7 Roll out the dough and place it inside a round mold. Prick the base using a fork and add the stew in the middle.

8 Cover with more dough and prick again so that the dough doesn't blow out during the baking step.

9 Brush on a little olive oil and bake at 180°C (350°F) until the surface is nicely browned.

10 Take the pie out of the mold and serve it hot.

Basil and artichoke pizza

6 people ¦ 50 minutes ¦ Difficulty *

Ingredients

For the dough:

150 g (5.3 oz) of wheat flour—about 1 ½ cup

100 g (3.5 fl oz) of water—about ½ cup

1 teaspoon of salt

1 teaspoon of sugar

15 g (½ an ounce) of fresh yeast

1 tablespoon of olive oil

For the topping:

4 tablespoons of crushed tomatoes

4 fresh tomatoes

1 green onion

12 artichokes in oil

2 tablespoons of olive oil

A pinch of salt

A pinch of pepper

Basil leaves

1 In a bowl, mix the flour, water, salt, sugar, yeast, and the olive oil.

2 Knead the dough thoroughly on a hard surface and let it rest for 20 minutes.

3 Dust the surface with a bit of flour and roll out the dough. Place it on a pizza pan.

4 Prick the dough with a fork and cover with the crushed tomatoes.

5 Bake the dough for 5 minutes at 180°C (355°F).

6 Remove the dough from the oven.

7 Cut the tomatoes into slices. Peel and cut the onion into thin strips. Cut the artichokes in half.

8 Top the pizza with slices of tomato, onion, the artichokes, olive oil, salt, and pepper.

9 Bake at 180°C (350°F) for 15 minutes. Serve the pizza with the basil leaves.

Dried tomato and cashew cheese pizza

6 people ┆ 30 minutes ┆ Difficulty ✳

Ingredients

For the dough:

150 g (5.3 oz) of wheat flour—about 1 ½ cup

100 g (3.5 fl oz) of water—about ½ cup

1 teaspoon of salt

1 teaspoon of sugar

15 g (½ an ounce) of fresh yeast

1 tablespoon of olive oil

For the cheese:

100 g (3.5 oz) of cashews

400 ml (about 14 fl oz) of water

2 tablespoons of brewer's yeast

1 teaspoon of salt

4 tablespoons of crushed tomatoes

For the topping:

6 cherry tomatoes

12 dried tomatoes

18 arugula leaves

Oregano leaves

1 In a bowl, mix the flour, water, salt, sugar, yeast, and the olive oil.

2 Knead the dough thoroughly on a hard surface and let it rest for 20 minutes.

3 Dust the surface with a bit of flour and roll out the dough. Place it on a pizza pan.

4 Prick the dough with a fork and cover with the crushed tomatoes.

5 Bake the dough for 5 minutes at 180°C (350°F).

6 Remove the dough from the oven.

7 To make the cheese, blend the cashews, the water, the brewer's yeast, and salt in an electric blender until you have a smooth sauce with no lumps.

8 Cut the cherry tomatoes in half and the dried tomatoes into thin strips.

9 Top the pizza with the cashew cheese, the dried tomatoes, the cherry tomatoes, and the arugula. Bake at 180°C (350°F) for 15 minutes.

10 Take the pizza out of the oven and serve with the fresh oregano leaves.

DESSERTS:

Brownies

6 people ┊ 1 hour ┊ Difficulty ✳

Ingredients

300 g (10.5 oz) of flour—about 2 ⅝ cups

1 teaspoon of salt

350 g (about 12 oz) of brown sugar

1 teaspoon of baking powder

30 g (1 oz) of powdered cocoa

200 g (7 oz) of semisweet chocolate

200 g (7 oz) of margarine

250 ml (9 fl oz) of water

1 teaspoon of vanilla

50 g (about 2 oz) of walnuts

1 In a bowl, mix the flour, salt, sugar, the baking powder, and the cocoa powder.

2 Next, melt the chocolate and margarine together in a pot over medium heat.

3 Mix the flour with the melted chocolate, the water, the vanilla, and the walnuts.

4 Add the batter to a 20 x 40 cm (8 x 16 in) baking pan and bake at 150°C (300°F) for 50 minutes.

5 Let the brownies cool and then cut them into small rectangles.

Brownies are a type of chocolate cake common in the United States that was created thanks to a culinary accident: it is said that towards the end of the nineteenth century, a North American cook was making a cake and forgot to add a leavening agent.

A good trick

Brownies *should be crunchy on the outside and soft on the inside. For this reason, it is important to control the baking time to avoid excessively drying them out*

Chocolate chip cookies

6 people ┆ 30 minutes ┆ Difficulty ✳

Ingredients

50 g (about 3 oz) of candied oranges

300 g (10.5 oz) of flour

1 teaspoon of salt

200 g (7 oz) of brown sugar

½ teaspoon of baking soda

100 g (3.5 oz) of chocolate chips—about ½ cup

300 g (10.5 oz) of margarine—about 2 ½ sticks

1 teaspoon of vanilla

1 Finely chop the candied oranges using a knife.

2 In a bowl, mix the flour, salt, sugar, the baking soda.

3 Add the chocolate chips, the margarine, and the vanilla. Mix well until you have a firm dough.

4 Shape several cookies and place them on a cookie sheet.

5 Bake at 180°C (350°F) until the edges of the cookies are golden brown. Let them cool on a rack and serve.

If you prefer...

To make **candied oranges,** you need 1 orange, 250 g (8 oz) of sugar, and 200 g (7 fl oz) of water. Slice the oranges and boil them over low heat along with the sugar and water for 2 hours, approximately.

Chocolate Chip Cookies is the name given to round cookies with chocolate chips. Eaten often in English-speaking countries, there are an unending number of variations.

Chocolate and banana muffins

6 people ┊ 30 minutes ┊ Difficulty *

Ingredients

310 g (11 oz) of flour—about 2 ¾ cups

280 g (10 oz) of brown sugar—about 1 ¼ cups

80 g (about 3 oz) of powdered cocoa

1 teaspoon of baking powder

1 teaspoon of salt

½ teaspoon of baking soda

270 ml (9 fl oz) of water

1 teaspoon of vanilla

180 g (6.3 oz) of sunflower oil

1 banana

1 In a bowl, mix the flour, sugar, cocoa powder, the baking powder, the baking soda, and the salt.

2 Add the water, vanilla, and sunflower oil and mix well until you have a smooth, uniform batter.

3 Thinly slice the banana and add it carefully to the batter.

4 Add the batter to small cupcake molds and bake at 180°C (350°F) until they are done.

The origin of muffins dates back to eighteenth century England. The name comes from the original *moofin*, an adaptation of the French term *moufflet* (soft bread).

✓ *A good trick*
If you insert a small wooden toothpick into the muffin and it comes out dry, then they are ready to come out of the oven.

If you prefer...
You can use a different kind of fruit when making **muffins**. They are also delicious with blackberries, blueberries, raspberries, or apples. (Also in this picture, lemon muffins.)

Lemon muffins

10 people ¦ 30 minutes ¦ Difficulty ✻

Ingredients

380 g (13.4 oz) of flour—about 3 ½ cups

280 g (10 oz) of brown sugar—about 1 ¼ cups

1 teaspoon of baking powder

½ teaspoon of baking soda

1 teaspoon of salt

270 ml (9 fl oz) of water

1 teaspoon of liquid vanilla

200 g (7 oz) of sunflower oil

3 lemons

225 g (8 oz) of powdered sugar

75 g (2.6 fl oz) of lemon juice—1 large or 2 small lemons

1 In a bowl, mix the flour, sugar, the baking powder, baking soda, and salt.

2 Add the water, vanilla, and sunflower oil. Mix well until you have a smooth, uniform batter.

3 Grate the rind of the lemons and add them to the batter.

4 Add the batter to small cupcake molds and bake at 180°C (350°F) until they are done.

5 To make the lemon glaze, mix the powdered sugar with the lemon juice and whisk well until there are no lumps.

6 Finish by covering the muffins with the glaze.

✓ *No mixer*

One of the differences between madeleines and muffins is that the latter doesn't require beating the ingredients as much. This way, the result is a less spongy and denser dough, which is characteristic of muffins.

* photo on previous page

Hazelnut crumble

5 people ¦ 20 minutes ¦ Difficulty ✳

Ingredients

100 g (3.5 oz) of wheat flour—about ¾ cup

100 g (3.5 oz) of brown sugar—about ½ cup

100 g (3.5 oz) of hazelnut flour—about ¾ cup

100 g (3.5 oz) of margarine—about 1 stick

1 teaspoon of salt

1 Mix all the ingredients in a bowl.

2 Crumble the dough with the help of a grater and put the small bits of dough on a baking tray.

3 Bake for 8 minutes at 180°C (350°F).

Hazelnut flour is an excellent source of protein and fiber. You can use it to make all kinds of cakes, cookies, and breads.

* photo on page 203

Apple crumble

10 people ¦ 40 minutes ¦ Difficulty ✳

Ingredients

5 apples—Golden
Delicious, preferred

Juice of 2 lemons

1 teaspoon of cinnamon

100 g (3.5 oz) of wheat
flour—about ¾ cup

100 g (3.5 oz) of
almond flour—about
½ cup

100 g (3.5 oz) of brown
sugar—about ½ cup

100 g (3.5 oz) of
margarine—about 1 stick

1 teaspoon of salt

1 Peel and dice the apples. Add the fruit to a tray and coat it with the lemon juice and cinnamon.

2 In a bowl, mix the different flours, sugar, margarine, and salt.

3 Crumble the dough with the help of a grater and sprinkle it over the apples.

4 Bake at 180°C (350°F) until the surface of the crumble starts to brown.

Crumbles are a typical English pie made from all kinds of fruit, like apples, grapes, plums, pears, etc. It is thought that this dessert was born during World War II, due to the rationing of food that was going on in the United Kingdom during the drawn-out conflict.

Almond and orange
blossom sablé

5 people ┆ 20 minutes ┆ Difficulty ✳

Ingredients

100 g (3.5 oz) of wheat flour—about ¾ cup
100 g (3.5 oz) of brown sugar—about ½ cup
100 g (3.5 oz) of almond flour—about ½ cup
100 g (3.5 oz) of margarine—about 1 stick
1 teaspoon of salt
1 teaspoon of orange rind

1 Mix all the ingredients in a bowl.

2 Roll the dough out between two pieces of parchment paper.

3 Using a cookie cutter, cut out several pieces of dough (about 4 cm, or 1.5 in, in diameter) and place them on another tray.

4 Bake at 180°C (350°F) for 8 minutes.

Sablé, or shortcrust, pastry is used as a base to make all kinds of cookies, and sweet and salty tarts, such as quiches and tartlets. In France, it is called sablé (sand) because of its grainy consistency.

Chocolate
sablé

5 people ┆ 20 minutes ┆ Difficulty ✳

Ingredients

70 g (2.5 oz) of wheat flour—about ½ cup
30 g (1 oz) of powdered cocoa—about ¼ cup
100 g (3.5 oz) of brown sugar—about ½ cup
100 g (3.5 oz) of almond flour—about ½ cup
100 g (3.5 oz) of margarine—about 1 stick
1 teaspoon of salt
1 teaspoon of vanilla

1 Mix all the ingredients in a bowl.

2 Using a roller, roll out the dough between two pieces of parchment paper.

3 Using a cookie cutter, cut out several pieces of dough (about 4 cm, or 1.5 in, in diameter) and place them on another tray.

4 Bake at 180°C (350°F) for 8 minutes.

✓ *A good trick*
It is helpful to let the dough rest before using it, because it will be much more malleable.

Hazelnut Crumble, Almond and Orange Blossom Sablé, and Chocolate Sablé

Carrot
and walnut cake

10 people ¦ 50 minutes ¦ Difficulty **

Ingredients

300 g (10.5 oz) of whole-wheat flour—about 3 cups

1 teaspoon of salt

270 g (9.5 oz) of brown sugar—about 1 ¼ cups

1 teaspoon of cinnamon

1 teaspoon of baking soda

1 teaspoon of baking powder

300 g (10.5 oz) of carrots—about 1 ½ cups

180 g (6.3 oz) of sunflower oil—about ¾ cup

200 ml (about 7 fl oz) of water

1 teaspoon of vanilla

130 g (4.5 oz) of walnuts—about ½ cup

For the orange icing:

300 g (10.5 oz) of powdered sugar—about 2 ¾ cups

100 g (3.5 fl oz) of orange juice—about ½ cup

1 In a bowl, mix the flour, salt, sugar, cinnamon, baking soda, and baking powder.

2 Peel, cut, and finely grate the carrots.

3 Add the oil, water, vanilla, carrots, and nuts to the mixture. Whisk until you have a uniform batter.

4 Put the batter in a Bundt pan and bake at 180°C (350°F) until it is done.

5 Insert a wooden toothpick into the cake to confirm that it is done cooking.

6 To make the orange icing, mix the powdered sugar with the orange juice and whisk well until there are no lumps.

7 Cover the cake with the icing and serve.

Blueberry loaf cake

6 people ¦ 45 minutes ¦ Difficulty *

Ingredients

175 g (about 6 oz) of flour— about 1 ½ cups

140 g (5 oz) of brown sugar—about ⅝ cup

½ teaspoon of baking powder

½ teaspoon of baking soda

½ teaspoon of salt

140 ml (5 fl oz) of water

Juice of 2 lemons

1 teaspoon of vanilla

140 g (5 oz) of sunflower oil

100 g (3.5 oz) of blueberries—about ½ cup

1 In a bowl, mix the flour, sugar, the baking powder, baking soda, and salt.

2 Add the water, lemon juice, vanilla, and sunflower oil. Whisk well until you have a uniform and smooth batter.

3 Add the blueberries and carefully mix.

4 Pour the batter into a loaf cake pan and bake at 180°C (350°F) until it is done.

If you prefer...
As an alternative to
blueberries, you can use
raspberries, which will be
delicious next to the
fresh, acidic flavor of
the lemon.

Chocolate mousse spheres

6 people ¦ 10 minutes ¦ Difficulty ✳

Ingredients

100 g (3.5 oz) of soy milk—about ½ cup

1 vanilla bean

225 g (8 oz) of dark chocolate

125 g (4.5 oz) of vegan whipping cream or milk—about ½ cup

Orange blossom water (if available), or substitute ½ teaspoon orange rind

25 g (1 oz) of margarine

Additional melted chocolate

Cocoa powder

1 In a pot, melt the chocolate into the whipping cream. Bring to boil.

2. Meanwhile, pour soy milk into in an electric blender cup. Scrape the seeds from the vanilla bean into the soy milk.

3. Add the boiling cream and emulsify on low speed.

4. Incorporate the orange blossom water and the margarine. Continue blending until you obtain a very fine emulsion.

5. Pour the mixture into a tray and refrigerate for at least 6 hours, allowing it to set.

6. Cut cubes of the desired size and roll them into spheres.

7. Dip spheres in additional melted chocolate and dust with cocoa powder.

If you prefer...

*If you don't like the taste of the **orange blossom water**, you can substitute if for an infusion of aromatic herbs (mint, oregano, etc.).*

Raisin shots

6 people ¦ 30 minutes ¦ Difficulty **

Ingredients

200 g (7 oz) of raisins—about 1 cup

50 ml (about ¼ cup) of rum

1 orange

500 ml (about 2 cups) of soy milk

80 g (about 3 oz) of sugar

30 g (1 oz) of cornstarch

1 In a saucepan, add the raisins, cover them with water, and add the shot of rum. Boil for about 30 minutes over low heat and set aside in small glasses.

2 Grate the rind of the orange.

3 Boil the milk with the sugar and add the orange rind.

4 In a bowl, dissolve the cornstarch in a little water. Add to milk mixture and warm over low heat for 2 minutes, stirring the whole time.

5 Add the orange crème Anglaise to each small glass, careful not to mix with the raisins too much, to create a couple of well defined layers.

6 Store in the refrigerator for a few hours.

7 Before serving, decorate with an orange slice (blood orange).

Soy milk is a vegetable liquid that contains no lactose, casein (lactic protein), vitamin B12, saturated fats, or cholesterol, and has less sodium and calories than cow's milk.

Cherry sponge cake

6 people ¦ 50 minutes ¦ Difficulty **

Ingredients

150 g (5.3 oz) of wheat flour—about 1 ⅓ cups

110 g (about 4 oz) of sugar—about ½ cup

1 teaspoon of baking soda

¼ teaspoon of baking powder

½ teaspoon of salt

30 g (1 oz) of cornstarch

100 ml (about ½ a cup) of sunflower oil

Juice of 2 lemons

140 ml (5 fl oz) of oat milk (substitute other grain or nut milk, optional)

300 g (10.5 oz) of cherries—pitted and canned, optional

10 g (2 teaspoons) of pectin

150 g (about 5 oz) of sugar—about ⅔ cup

1 In a bowl, mix the wheat flour, sugar, the baking soda, baking powder, salt, and cornstarch.

2 Add the oil, the juice of the lemons, and the oat milk. Mix well until you have a smooth batter.

3 Pour the mixture into a mold and bake at 170°C (350°F) until the batter is well cooked. Store in a cold place.

4 Next, pit the cherries and blend the pulp using a hand blender.

5 In a pot, boil the blended cherries.

6 Mix the pectin with the sugar and add it bit by bit to the cherries. Stir constantly to keep it from sticking and wait for it to come to a boil.

7 Place the cherry marmalade on top of the cake and let it cool for 3 hours in the refrigerator.

» **Oat milk** is one of the tastiest vegetable drinks you can find. It is rich in fiber, helps reduce cholesterol, and helps gut flora, as well as digestive functions in general.

» **Pectin** is a coagulating ingredient often used for making marmalade, jams, and jellies. It is naturally extracted from vegetable matter.

Raspberry and rose petal loaf cake

6 people ¦ 30 minutes ¦ Difficulty ✳

Ingredients

- 200 g (7 oz) of wheat flour—1 ¾ cups
- 1 teaspoon of salt
- 120 g (4 oz) of brown sugar
- 50 g (about 2 oz) of cornstarch
- 2 teaspoons of baking powder
- 125 ml (½ cup) of sunflower oil
- 80 ml (about 3 fl oz) of water—about ⅓ cup
- 60 ml (2 fl oz) of rose water
- 10 fresh raspberries

1 In a bowl, mix the flour, salt, sugar, cornstarch, and the baking powder.

2 Add the oil, water, and rose water. Blend well until you have a smooth, uniform batter.

3 Put the batter into a loaf cake pan and push the raspberries into the interior of the batter.

4 Bake at 180°C (350°F) until it is done.

» **Sunflower oil** is a healthy choice thanks to its content of unsaturated fats and vitamin E, as well as its power as an antioxidant. Eating it helps reduce levels of cholesterol and triglycerides in the blood.

» **Raspberries** are one of the fruits with the lowest amount of calories (only 32 for every 100 g, or 3.5 oz). They are rich in manganese, iron, magnesium, phosphorus, calcium, and potassium.

» **Rose water** is obtained via the process of distilling the rose petals, and, thanks to its intense flavor and aroma, is used to make all kinds of desserts.

✓ *Be careful . . .*

When inserting a wooden toothpick to verify that the cake is done, you might pierce a raspberry and get confused, since the tip will probably come out moist. In this case, you should insert another toothpick to be sure.

Chocolate cookies

12 people ┆ 20 minutes ┆ Difficulty ✳

Ingredients

280 g (10 oz) of wheat flour—about 2 ½ cups

1 teaspoon of salt

½ teaspoon of baking soda

50 g (about 2 oz) of powdered cocoa

225 g (8 oz) of margarine

220 g (about 8 oz) of brown sugar

85 g (3 oz) of dark chocolate

1 teaspoon of vanilla

1 In a bowl, mix the flour, salt, baking soda, and cocoa powder.

2 In another dish, mix the margarine and the sugar.

3 Add the flour to the bowl with the margarine and mix the dough, careful not to work it too much so your cookies come out soft.

4 Chop the chocolate into small pieces and add it to the dough alongside the vanilla. Mix well.

5 Shape and add several cookies to a cookie sheet and bake at 180°C (350°F) for 10 minutes.

Sachertorte

12 people ¦ 40 minutes ¦ Difficulty ✳✳✳

Ingredients

300 g (10.5 oz) of wheat flour—2 ⅜ cups

1 teaspoon of salt

225 g (8 oz) of brown sugar

60 g (about 2 oz) of powdered cocoa—about ¼ cup

1 teaspoon of baking soda

2 teaspoons of baking powder

250 ml (9 fl oz) of water

130 ml (about ½ a cup) of sunflower oil

Apricot

marmalade

200 g (7 oz) of dark chocolate

150 g (just over 5 oz) of margarine—about 1 stick plus 1 tablespoon

50 g (about 2 oz) of sunflower oil

1 In a bowl, mix the wheat flour, salt, sugar, cocoa, baking soda, and baking powder.

2 Add the water and the oil and whisk well until you have a smooth and uniform batter.

3 Divide the batter into 3 round molds (20 cm, or 8 in, in diameter) and bake at 180°C (350°F) until it's done. Store in a cold place.

4 Spread the marmalade over 2 of the cake sections and stack all 3 pieces on top of each other, putting the piece with no marmalade on top. Freeze the cake.

5 Melt the chocolate in a double boiler along with the margarine and the oil. Emulsify using a hand blender.

6 Place the cake on a rack and completely cover it with the melted chocolate.

Catalonian cream

6 people ┊ 10 minutes ┊ Difficulty *

Ingredients

¼ teaspoon of agar agar

500 ml (about 2 cups) of soy milk

1 stick of cinnamon

Zest of 1 lemon

Zest of 1 orange

80 g (about 3 oz) of sugar

20 g (4 teaspoons) of corn flour

Sugar for caramelizing

1 Submerge the agar agar in the soy milk until it completely dissolves.

2 Add the cinnamon, the grated rind of the lemon and orange, and the sugar. Bring the mixture to a boil.

3 Dissolve the flour into a bit of water and add it to the milk.

4 In a pot, heat the mixture over low heat, stirring constantly, for couple of minutes.

5 Divide the cream among 6 bowls and let it cool in the refrigerator.

6 Sprinkle it with a bit of sugar and caramelize it before serving.

Catalonian cream is a desert that is usually made with cow's milk and eggs. The vegan alternative is simple, and the outcome is equally tasty. It is sufficient to replace those ingredients with soy milk and agar agar. This last component helps to give this dessert a firm and creamy texture.

Flapjacks

12 people ¦ 15 minutes ¦ Difficulty ✽

Ingredients

200 g (7 oz) of margarine

150 ml (5 fl oz) of maple syrup—about ⅝ cup

350 g (1 ½ cups) of oats

1 In a double boiler, melt the margarine and mix it with the maple syrup and oats.

2 Place the mixture in a baking dish.

3 Bake at 150°C (300°F) until the edges start to look well browned.

4 Cool it in the fridge for 3 hours and, finally, cut it into rectangles before serving.

Flapjacks are small cereal bars that originate from English cooking. They are usually made with oats, but you can also use all kinds of nuts, raisins, dried apricots . . . They are perfect for breakfast or a snack for the little ones.

If you prefer...
You can use agave
syrup so that the **flapjacks**
don't come out as sweet.
But that depends on your taste
for sweet flavors.

Flapjacks with vanilla frosting

12 people ┆ 15 minutes ┆ Difficulty ✳

Ingredients

200 g (7 oz) of margarine

100 ml (3.5 fl oz) of maple syrup—about ½ cup

350 g (1 ½ cups) of oats

For frosting:

70 g (2 ½ oz) of margarine—about ½ stick or 5 tablespoons

200 g (7 oz) of powdered sugar

1 teaspoon of vanilla

1 In a double boiler, melt the margarine and mix it with the maple syrup and oats.

2 Next, place the mixture in a baking dish.

3 Bake at 150°C (300°F) until the edges start to look well browned. Store in the refrigerator.

4 To make frosting, mix the margarine, sugar, and vanilla in a bowl.

5 Finally, spread the mixture over the flapjacks and cut them into rectangles.

Plum sponge cake with hazelnuts and almonds

12 people ¦ 30 minutes ¦ Difficulty ✻

Ingredients

320 g (about 11 oz) of wheat flour—about 3 cups

1 teaspoon of salt

270 g (8 oz) of sugar

2 teaspoons of baking powder

1 teaspoon of cinnamon

180 ml (¾ a cup) of sunflower oil

250 ml (1 cup) of soy milk

120 g (4 oz) of plums—about 2 large plums

50 g (about 2 oz) of hazelnuts—about ¼ cup

50 g (about 2 oz) of almonds—about ¼ cup

1 In a bowl, mix the flour, salt, sugar, baking powder, and the cinnamon.

2 Add the oil and the milk. Mix well until you have a smooth and uniform batter.

3 Add the plums, the hazelnuts, and the almonds.

4 Pour the batter into a rectangular pan, dust it on top with sugar, and bake it at 180°C (350°F) until it is done.

Light sponge cake

6 people ¦ 25 minutes ¦ Difficulty ✳

Ingredients

200 g (7 oz) of wheat flour—1 ¾ cups

½ teaspoon of salt

1 teaspoon of baking soda

1 teaspoon of baking powder

1 teaspoon of cinnamon

80 ml (⅓ cup) of agave syrup

90 ml (6 tbsp) of sunflower oil

110 ml (½ cup) of rice milk—other grain or nut milk optional

1 In a bowl, mix the flour, salt, baking soda, baking powder, and the cinnamon.

2 Add the syrup, the oil, and the rice milk. Mix well until you have a smooth, uniform batter.

3 Put the batter in a small pan and bake at 150°C (300°F) until it is done.

» **Agave syrup** is a sweet vegetable juice that is extracted from a species of cactus native to the tropical Americas and the Caribbean. It has twice the sweetening power of common sugar, thanks to its high fructose and glucose content.

» **Rice milk** is a vegetable drink highly recommended for people suffering from gastric disorders or slow and heavy digestion.

Blueberry scones

6 people ┆ 25 minutes ┆ Difficulty ✳

Ingredients

370 g (13 oz) of wheat flour—about 3 ¼ cups

130 g (4.5 oz) of sugar

1 tablespoon of baking powder

A pinch of salt

120 g (4 oz) of margarine—1 stick

130 ml (½ cup) of water

Zest of 2 lemons

100 g (3.5 oz) of blueberries—about ½ cup

1 In a bowl, mix the flour, sugar, the baking powder, and a pinch of salt.

2 Add the margarine and knead until you have a crumbly consistency.

3 Add the water and the zest of the lemons. Continue kneading the mixture.

4 Add the blueberries and form the dough into a disk.

5 Cut the dough into sixths and bake at 180°C (350°F) for 20 minutes.

» Scones are delicious, traditional English cakes that are usually made with berries like raspberries or blueberries.

» The best time to buy blueberries starts in the month of June and lasts until December. When purchasing, you should look for a bright, shiny skin tone, and pick out the more fragrant berries.

» Baking powder is used to increase the volume of dough and is particularly useful for making cakes. It is more effective than baking soda, since it starts acting at a lower temperature and is completely tasteless.

Coconut balls

6 people ¦ 30 minutes (plus 2 minutes to cool) ¦ Difficulty *

Ingredients

½ cup of coconut oil
1 cup of grated coconut
1 cup of almond flour
½ cup of agave syrup
¼ teaspoon of salt
Grated coconut for dredging

1 Add the coconut oil to a double boiler and heat until it becomes a smooth liquid.

2 In a bowl, mix the cup of grated coconut, the flour, syrup, coconut oil, and salt until you have a uniform, firm dough.

3 Shape the dough into small balls and dredge them in grated coconut.

4 Let them chill in the refrigerator for a couple of hours and serve them cold.

Coconut oil is a very tasty and aromatic vegetable oil. It is rich in lauric acid, a component found in mother's milk. Aside from its culinary uses, it is an excellent ingredient for making soap and all kinds of natural and homemade cosmetics.

Strawberry flan

6 people ¦ 20 minutes ¦ Difficulty ✳

Ingredients

500 ml (about 2 cups) of rice milk

80 g (3 oz) of agave syrup—about ⅓ cup

1 vanilla bean

40 g (1.5 oz) of corn flour

1 teaspoon of liquid caramel (for flan)

36 strawberries (6 per person)

100 g (3.5 oz) of sugar—about ½ cup

Chocolate shavings

1 Boil the rice milk with the agave syrup and the vanilla bean (split down the middle and seedless).

2 Add the flour, diluted in a bit of water, and boil over low heat for 3 minutes.

3 Spread a layer of caramel in the bottom of 6 small jello molds.

4 Add the drained mixture to the jello molds and keep cold for 5 hours.

5 Puree a dozen strawberries, add the sugar, and boil for 3 minutes.

6 Add the syrup on top of the 24 remaining strawberries and store in the refrigerator.

7 Turn out the flans and serve with some strawberries and previously grated chocolate.

Green tea and maple syrup cupcakes

6 people ¦ 45 minutes ¦ Difficulty **

Ingredients

120 g (4 oz) of wheat flour—about 1 ⅛ cups

½ teaspoon of salt

30 g (1 oz) of cornstarch—4 tablespoons

1 teaspoon of baking powder

1 tablespoon of green tea, Matcha preferred

100 ml (about ½ cup) of water

95 ml (6.5 tbsp) of maple syrup

1 teaspoon of vanilla

90 ml (6 tbsp) of sunflower oil

For the cream:

60 g (2 oz) of non-hydrogenated vegetable margarine

130 g (4.5 oz) of powdered sugar—about ½ cup

½ teaspoon of green tea, Matcha preferred

1 tablespoon of soy milk

1 In a bowl, mix the flour, salt, cornstarch, the baking powder, and the Matcha tea.

2 Add the water, maple syrup, vanilla, and the sunflower oil.

3 Whisk the mixture until you have a smooth, uniform batter.

4 Add the batter to 6 small cupcake molds and bake at 180°C (350°F) until the cupcakes are done. Insert a wooden toothpick into the cupcakes to confirm that they are done.

5 Let them chill in the refrigerator for 3 hours.

6 In another bowl, mix the margarine, powdered sugar, green tea, and the milk.

7 Vigorously whisk until the cream no longer has any lumps.

8 Put the cream in a pastry bag and decorate each cupcake.

Cupcakes are small cakes typical to the United States. Their name is due to the fact that in the past, there were no appropriate molds and so they were served in cups. Thanks to their appearance in the series "Sex and the City," they've become very popular outside of that country. These small cakes are usually decorated very prettily, with different layers of colors and shapes.

Mango and amaretto cupcakes

6 people ¦ 1 hour ¦ Difficulty **

Ingredients

160 g (5.6 oz) of wheat flour—1 ⅜ cups

½ teaspoon of salt

120 g (4 oz) of brown sugar—about ½ cup

10 g (a rounded tablespoon) of cornstarch

¼ teaspoon of baking soda

1 teaspoon of baking powder

110 ml (about ½ cup) of water

½ teaspoon of vanilla extract

90 ml (6 tbsp) of sunflower oil

½ a mango

½ cup of amaretto

For the cream:

60 g (2 oz) of non-hydrogenated vegetable margarine—½ stick

140 g (5 oz) of powdered sugar—1 ¼ cups

6 tablespoons of amaretto

1 In a bowl, mix the flour, salt, sugar, cornstarch, and the baking soda, and baking powder.

2 Add the water, vanilla, and sunflower oil.

3 Peel and finely dice the mango and add it to the batter.

4 Whisk the mixture until you have a smooth, uniform batter.

5 Add the batter to 6 small cupcake molds and bake at 180°C (350°F) until the cupcakes are done. Insert a wooden toothpick into the cupcakes to confirm that they are done.

6 Take them out of the oven and cover each cupcake with a tablespoon of amaretto and let them chill in the refrigerator for 3 hours.

7 In another bowl, mix the margarine, powdered sugar, and the amaretto.

8 Vigorously whisk until the cream no longer has any lumps.

9 Put the cream in a pastry bag and decorate each cupcake.

Amaretto is an Italian liquor made from apricots and almonds. Its unique aroma and flavor tends to pair well with all kinds of sweet dishes.

Cappuccino cupcakes

6 people ¦ 1 hour ¦ Difficulty **

Ingredients

110 g (about 4 oz) of wheat flour—about 1 cup

60 g (2 oz) of cornstarch—4 tablespoons

20 g (about 1 oz) of powdered cocoa—about ⅛ cup

1 tablespoon of instant coffee

120 g (4 oz) of brown sugar—about ⅝ cup

½ teaspoon of salt

1 teaspoon of baking powder

½ teaspoon of baking soda

110 ml (about ½ cup) of water

½ teaspoon of vanilla extract

100 ml (about ½ a cup) of sunflower oil

For the cream:

60 g (2 oz) of non-hydrogenated vegetable margarine—½ stick

140 g (5 oz) of powdered sugar—1 ¼ cups

1 tablespoon of ground coffee

1 In a bowl, mix the flour, cornstarch, cocoa, coffee, sugar, salt, baking powder, and baking soda.

2 Add the water, vanilla, and sunflower oil.

3 Whisk the mixture until you have a smooth, uniform batter.

4 Add the batter to 6 small cupcake molds and bake at 180°C (350°F) until the cupcakes are done. Insert a wooden toothpick into the cupcakes to confirm that they are done.

5 Let them chill in the refrigerator for 3 hours.

6 In another bowl, mix the margarine, powdered sugar, and the ground coffee.

7 Vigorously whisk until the cream no longer has any lumps.

8 Put the cream in a pastry bag and decorate each cupcake.

9 Finish by dusting the cupcakes with a bit of cocoa powder.

Green tea and maple syrup cupcake

Cappuccino cupcake

Mango and amaretto cupcake

"everyones favourite party cake"

Rose and raspberry cupcakes

6 people ¦ 45 minutes ¦ Difficulty **

Ingredients

150 g (5.3 oz) of wheat flour—about 1 ⅓ cups

½ teaspoon of salt

110 g (about 4 oz) of brown sugar—about ½ cup

10 g (a rounded tablespoon) of cornstarch

¼ teaspoon of baking soda

1 teaspoon of baking powder

100 ml (about ½ cup) of soy milk

20 ml (4 tsp) of rose water

½ teaspoon of vanilla extract

85 ml (about ⅓ cup) of sunflower oil

125 g (4.5 oz) of raspberries—about ½ cup

For the cream:

60 g (2 oz) of non-hydrogenated vegetable margarine—½ stick

140 g (5 oz) of powdered sugar—1 ¼cups

1 tablespoon of rose water

1 In a bowl, mix the flour, salt, sugar, cornstarch, the baking soda, and baking powder.

2 Add the soy milk, the rose water, vanilla, and the sunflower oil.

3 Whisk the mixture until you have a smooth, uniform batter.

4 Add the batter to 6 small cupcake molds and insert 3 raspberries inside each cupcake (press the berries in with your fingers). Bake at 180°C (350°F) until the cupcakes are done. Insert a wooden toothpick into the cupcakes to confirm.

5 Let them chill in the refrigerator for 3 hours.

6 In another bowl, mix the margarine, powdered sugar, and the rose water.

7 Vigorously whisk until the cream no longer has any lumps.

8 Put the cream into a pasty bag and decorate each cupcake.

9 Finish by garnishing with one rose petal.

If you prefer...

*To make **rose water** at home, boil 2 cups of water, add 1 cup of rose petals, and let them infuse for 30 minutes. Strain out the petals and chill.*

Chocolate strawberry cupcakes

6 people ¦ 45 minutes ¦ Difficulty **

Ingredients

120 g (4 oz) of wheat flour—about 1 ⅛ cups

½ teaspoon of salt

130 g (4.5 owz) of brown sugar—about ⅔ cup

10 g (a rounded tablespoon) of cornstarch

½ teaspoon of baking soda

1 teaspoon of baking powder

120 ml (½ cup) of water

½ teaspoon of vanilla extract

90 ml (6 tbsp) of sunflower oil

60 g (2 oz) of strawberries—about ¼ cup

For the cream:

60 g (2 oz) of non-hydrogenated vegetable margarine—½ stick

160 g (5.5 oz) of powdered sugar—about 1 ⅜ cups

3 tablespoons of soy milk

1 teaspoon of vanilla extract

100g (3.5 oz) of semi-sweet chocolate

1 In a bowl, mix the flour, salt, sugar, cornstarch, the baking soda, and baking powder.

2 Add the water, vanilla, and sunflower oil.

3 Cut the strawberries into small pieces and add them to the batter.

4 Whisk the mixture until you have a smooth, uniform batter.

5 Add the batter to 6 small cupcake molds and bake at 180°C (350°F) until the cupcakes are done. Insert a wooden toothpick into the cupcakes to confirm that they are done.

6 Let them chill in the refrigerator for 3 hours.

7 Melt the chocolate in a double boiler.

8 In another bowl, mix the margarine, powdered sugar, soy milk, vanilla, and melted chocolate.

9 Vigorously whisk until the cream no longer has any lumps.

10 Put the cream in a pastry bag and decorate each cupcake.

11 Finish decorating each cupcake with a small strawberry.

Treacle tart

6 people ¦ 40 minutes ¦ Difficulty **

Ingredients

170 g (6 oz) of
non-hydrogenated
vegetable margarine—
1 ½ sticks

80 g (3 oz) of powdered
sugar—about ¾ cup

200 g (7 oz) of wheat
flour—1 ¾ cups

For the filling:

300 g (10.5 oz) of maple
syrup—about 1 cup

3 lemons

180 g (about 6 oz) of
bread crumbs

1 In a bowl, mix the margarine, sugar, and flour. Knead for 5 minutes.

2 Put the dough into a pan. Cover it with parchment paper and place a few dry legumes on top to keep it from rising when it gets heated.

3 Bake at 180°C (350°F) for 15 minutes.

4 Take it out of the oven, let it cool, and remove the legumes and parchment paper.

5 In a saucepan, heat the maple syrup until it boils.

6 Grate two lemons and then juice them.

7 Add the bread crumbs, the zest, and the juice to the syrup. Stir well and pour it onto the crust.

8 Shape the leftover dough into strips and place them on top of the filling until it's totally covered. Decorate the surface with several slices of lemon.

9 Bake for 25–30 minutes at 170°C (350°F).

10 Let it chill in the refrigerator for 4 hours and serve.

Coconut and raspberry cookies

6 people ¦ 40 minutes ¦ Difficulty *

Ingredients

180 g (about 6 oz) of margarine—1 ½ sticks

120 g (4 oz) of sugar—about ½ cup

300 g (10.5 oz) of wheat flour—about 2 ⅝ cups

1 teaspoon of vanilla

45 g (1.5 oz) of powdered almonds—about ¼ cup

¼ teaspoon of salt

1 jar of raspberry marmalade

Grated coconut

1 In a bowl, mix the margarine, sugar, flour, vanilla, powdered almonds, and salt until you have a uniform dough.

2 Roll the dough out, dusting with a bit of flour so it doesn't stick. Using a cookie cutter, cut out small circles, about 7 cm (almost 3 in) in diameter.

3 Place the dough on a baking sheet covered in parchment paper and put it in the oven for 10 minutes at about 160°C (325°F).

4 Let the cookies rest at room temperature for 1 hour.

5 To make the filling, spread the raspberry marmalade onto one cookie, top it with another cookie, and dredge the edges in the grated coconut. Repeat this step with the other cookies.

6 Finally, put the cookies into the fridge for 2 hours and serve them chilled.

Lemon Tart

6 people ¦ 1 hour and 15 minutes ¦ Difficulty ✱✱✱

Ingredients

For the tartlets:

75 g (almost 3 oz) of non-hydrogenated margarine—⅓ cup

15 g (½ oz) of powdered almonds—about ⅛ cup

40 g (just over 1 oz) of powdered sugar—⅓ cup

130 g (4.5 oz) of wheat flour—1 ⅛ cups

For the filling:

2 lemons

100 ml (about ½ cup) of soy milk

120 g (4 oz) of sugar—about ½ cup

60 g (2 fl oz) of water—¼ cup

50 g (about 2 oz) of cornstarch—about ¼ cup

70 g (2.5 fl oz) of corn oil—about ⅓ cup

For the butter:

100 g (3.5 oz) of non-hydrogenated margarine—about 1 stick

200 g (7 oz) of powdered sugar—1 ¾ cups

1 lemon

1 Start by making the tartlets. In a bowl, mix the margarine, almonds, powdered sugar, and flour until you get a uniform dough. Cover the mixture with plastic wrap and store in the fridge for 2 hours.

2 Once cold, roll the dough out with a rolling pin, dusting with a bit of flour to keep it from sticking.

3 Place 6 small, round, bottomless baking molds on a baking sheet and put the dough inside them.

4 Cover the top of the molds with parchment paper and weigh them down with garbanzos to keep the dough from rising.

5 Bake at 150°C (300°F) for 15 minutes. Remove the garbanzos and parchment paper. Let it cool.

6 To make the filling, mix the zest and juice of the lemons with the soy milk and sugar. Cook over low heat.

7 In another pot, boil the water and cornstarch and add the lemon mixture. Stir well for a couple of minutes.

8 Remove the pot from the heat and add the oil.

9 Add the lemon filling to the tartlets and let them chill in the refrigerator for a couple of hours.

10 To make the butter, whisk the margarine and powdered sugar together until there are no more lumps. Add the lemon juice bit by bit, along with the zest. Put the butter in a pastry bag and decorate the tartlets.

Montserrat rocks

6 people ¦ 30 minutes ¦ Difficulty ✳

Ingredients

250 ml (1 cup) of soy milk

1 vanilla bean

100 g (3.5 oz) of maple syrup—about ⅓ cup

5 mint leaves

500 g (about 1 lb) of dark chocolate

100 g (3.5 oz) of powdered sugar— ⅞ cup

100 g (3.5 oz) of powdered cocoa— ⅞ cup

1 In a pot, boil the soy milk along with the vanilla bean (split down the middle and seedless), the maple syrup, and the mint leaves.

2 Take off of the heat, drain, and mix it with the chocolate. Emulsify the mixture using a hand blender until it achieves an oily texture. Chill in the fridge for 1 ½ hours.

3 In a separate bowl, mix the powdered sugar and powdered cocoa.

4 Shape the reserved chocolate into small truffles and dredge it in the cocoa mixture. Finally, chill them in the fridge and serve them cold.

Chocolate and coffee cake

6 people ¦ 1 hour ¦ Difficulty: Low **

Ingredients

For the cake:

150 g (5.3 oz) of wheat flour—1 ⅜ cups

½ teaspoon of salt

130 g (4.5 oz) of brown sugar—about ⅔ cup

1 teaspoon of baking soda

1 teaspoon of baking powder

40 g (about 1.5 oz) of powdered cocoa—⅓ cup

10 g (about 4 tsp) of instant coffee

120 g (4 oz) sunflower oil

125 ml (½ cup) soy milk

1 teaspoon liquid vanilla

For the cream:

200 g (7 oz) of non-hydrogenated margarine—1 ¾ stick

2 tablespoons of sunflower oil

100 g (3.5 oz) of dark chocolate

125 g (4.5 oz) of powdered sugar—1 ⅛ cups

1 teaspoon of instant coffee

4 tablespoons of hazelnut milk

1 In a bowl, mix the flour, salt, sugar, the baking soda, the baking powder, the cocoa, and the coffee.

2 Add the oil, soy milk, and liquid vanilla. Mix well until you get a uniform batter.

3 Add the batter to a round baking mold about 20 cm (8 in) in diameter and bake at 180°C (350°F) until the cake is done. Insert a wooden toothpick to confirm (if it comes out clean and dry, you may stop baking).

4 Let them chill in the refrigerator for 6 hours.

5 Melt the chocolate in a double boiler.

6 In another bowl, mix the margarine, the oil, the chocolate, and the powdered sugar. Using a whisk, vigorously mix until you achieve a cream without any lumps.

7 Slowly add the hazelnut milk and the instant coffee. Continue whisking vigorously.

8 Using a spatula or large knife, spread the chocolate cream over the cake.

9 Store in the fridge for 3 hours and serve chilled.

Non-hydrogenated margarine is a much healthier alternative to traditional margarine. This is thanks to its low, or null, content of hydrogenated or trans fat, which is harmful to cardiovascular health.

Hazelnut milk *is an excellent addition to your daily diet. It is rich in vitamins A and E, folic acid, calcium, magnesium, and fiber. Also, it contains very high quality vegetable proteins, ideal for those following a vegan diet.*

Banana lollipops

6 people ¦ 20 minutes ¦ Difficulty ✳

Ingredients

1 banana, sliced

12 long wooden skewers

150 g (just over 5 oz) of margarine—1 ¼ stick

200 g (7 oz) of dark chocolate

50 g (about 2 oz) of sunflower oil—about ¼ cup

50 g (about 2 oz) of nut brittle, almond preferred

1 Put one slice of banana on the end of each skewer and put them in the freezer.

2 In a double boiler, melt the margarine and chocolate.

3 Add the sunflower oil and mix well.

4 Dip the banana slices into the melted chocolate and add the almond brittle.

5 Serve chilled, but not frozen.

To make a simple home made almond brittle, just crush 100 g (3.5 oz or ¾ cup) of raw almonds and sauté them in a pan with 1 tablespoon of olive or sunflower oil. When they start to get toasted, add 1 tablespoon of sugar and mix well. When the sugar has dissolved, take the almonds off the heat and let them cool.

If you prefer...

You can substitute the almond brittle with a peanut, hazelnut, or pistachio brittle by crushing and toasting those nuts instead. The secret is to make sure the lollipops are nice and crunchy.

Rum and banana
milkshake

6 people ┆ 5 minutes ┆ Difficulty *

Ingredients

6 bananas
4 tablespoons of brown sugar
600 ml (2 ½ cups) of soy milk
250 ml (1 cup) of rum
50 g (about 2 oz) of raisins (¼ cup)

1 Peel and slice up the bananas.

2 Blend all the ingredients until you have a nice and creamy shake.

3 Let it chill and serve in 6 glasses.

Chocolate and
avocado milkshake

6 people ┆ 10 minutes ┆ Difficulty *

Ingredients

3 avocados, 80 g (3 oz) of brown sugar (⅓ cup),
1.2 l (5 cups) of soy milk, 1 tablespoon of powdered cocoa, 1 teaspoon of vanilla extract

1 Peel the avocados and reserve half.

2 Blend and mix the avocados with 600 ml (2 and ½cups) of soy milk and the sugar until the consistency is smooth and uniform.

3 Fill the glasses halfway up with the shake.

4 Mix the leftover milk with the cocoa, the vanilla extract, and the reserved avocado.

5 Add the mixture to each glass, careful not to agitate the structure of the liquid already in the glass. Serve chilled.

Raspberry and
elderberry milkshake

6 people ┆ 5 minutes ┆ Difficulty *

Ingredients

800 g (28 oz) of raspberries
5 elderberry flowers
(or 1 tablespoon elderberry syrup)
300 ml (1 ¼ cups) of soy milk
100 g (3.5 oz) of sugar
1 teaspoon of vanilla extract

1 Blend and mix all the ingredients until you are left with a smooth, uniform cream.

2 Serve in 6 glasses and decorate with elderberry or violet flowers (if available) and raspberries.

If you prefer...
You can use **elderberry flowers**
in all kinds of salads,
as an addition to sweet and
savory recipes, as well as
for making aromatic
infusions.

Recipe index

Also available from Skyhorse Publishing, Inc.

Vegan Cupcakes by Toni Rodríguez
Mouth-Watering Vegan Burgers by Toni Rodríguez

* * *

Café Paradiso Seasons by Denis Cotter
Cast Iron Cooking for Vegetarians by Joanna Pruess
Easy As Vegan Pie by Hannah Kaminsky
Linda McCartney's Home Vegetarian Cooking by Linda McCartney
Meatless Eats edited by Sarah James
No More Allergies Cookbook by Gary Null
The Squeeze by Karliin Brooks
The Vegan Cookie Connoisseur by Kelly Peloza
The Vegan Girl's Guide to Life by Melisser Elliott
The Vegetarian Chef by Susan Crowther
The Vegetarians' Bible by Inga-Britta Sundqvist
Vega a la Mode by Hannah Kaminsky
Vegan Desserts by Hannah Kaminsky
Vegan Dinner Party by Sandra Vungi
Vegan Vitality by Karina Inkster
Vegetarian Comfort Foods by Jennifer Browne
Vegetarian Entertaining by Jodi Moreno
Vegetarian Grilling by Karen Schulz and Maren Jahnke
Whole Bowls by Allison Day

My recipes

My recipes

My recipes

My recipes

My recipes

My recipes

My recipes

Thanks

After five years among stoves and bars, I have managed to write my first vegan cookbook. It has been a tough few years due to everything it has entailed: work, patience, discipline, early mornings, persistence, loans, crying, begging, good dishes, bad dishes, headaches, laughter, and from restaurant to restaurant, more work . . . but always with the support of many people during those moments.

I would like to thank Oceano publishing house, especially Jordi, Esther, and Pere, for their patience and excellent work. To Carla (www.IraMakeUp.com) for making the carrot cake the most well-known in the whole world, and for being the best model I've had. To Jonathan, for eating the edges of those brownies. To Balu, Cristian Torrent, Jose el gordo, Adri and her parents, to the Blisters on the fingers, to the Sexy Rockets, to Barbi, Marc Lenoir, to Adri, Eva, and Sara de Gopal, the Biocenter restaurant, to Chiara and Sara del Sésamo, to Pelucas (Pedro) and his Boom Boom Rest, Sonia Capo, Rosa, Salva y Whisky, to Javi Espiritual Chef for all that raw food that illuminates us and fills us with love. To Dani from the Vegania shop, to the girls from the coffee shop for giving me those afternoons with good coffee. Borja and Jordi, who are lost in the world of cinema and fame, I would like to thank with all my heart for all the support they've given me whenever I needed it. To Adriana and Jaume, from *Cocina Vegetariana* magazine, for giving me that big push. To the marvelous team of Becky Lawton, for putting up with me day after day, and for trusting that I would make this book a reality. To Francisco Vásquez and Leonora Esquivel, for making it possible for this world to be more fair to animals every day, for having watched me grow and supporting me in my culinary aspect from the first day, and for always being at my side when I needed them. You are incredible! To the person that has given me all her love and trust while I made this book: thank you, Alba. To Ana, Eduardo Padrós, Fran, Jenny, Dani, Gabriel, and Rose, for making my dream come true. I don't know what to say about my family, anything I say would be too little. They are always at my side when I need them and they know that I will always be there for whatever they need. To my aunts, cousins, my siblings Diana and Luis, Lupita, my first dog Cobi, and my father and mother, who are responsible for making me who I am.